Climbing the Retirement Mountain

AND GETTING SAFELY DOWN THE OTHER SIDE

Calvin Goetz and Andrew Rafal

Book layout ©2013 BookDesignTemplates.com

Climbing the Retirement Mountain/ Calvin Goetz and Andrew Rafal —1st ed.
ISBN 978-1541130937

Contents

I dedicate this book to my parents, Gary and Lorraine Goetz, who taught me the values of hard work, dedication and leadership that have led me to where I am today.
~ Calvin Goetz

Jules and Winter — you are the inspiration that guides me daily. Without you none of this would be possible. To the rest of my family — words cannot express how lucky I am to have you all in my life! There are so many more to thank, but that can wait until the next book.
~ Andrew Rafal

Preface

C amelback Mountain is a geological oddity that looms up out of the flat Phoenix cityscape as if to remind the concrete and glass city below that not all of the desert can be so easily tamed. The mountain is named for the two signature humps that do, if you squint and look at it from the proper angle, resemble the undulating back of a Bactrian camel heading west toward California.

We have an excellent view of this iconic landmark from almost anywhere in the Phoenix area. In fact, if you stand in the median and look eastward down the street on which our office buildings are located, it appears as if the street dead-ends at the base of the mountain – thus the name Camelback Road.

This sight inspired the comparisons between retiring and climbing a mountain, and you will see references to this scattered throughout the pages of this book. That may also explain the title. If we lived near the ocean, I'm sure we would have found some other source of inspiration, but the more we explored the idea, the more similarities we began to see between retiring and reaching a pinnacle, scaling a peak, climbing a mountain. Successful retirement is the quest of many Americans. Through our early working years, we tend to see retirement as some far off "someday" destination. Then, as the years bring us closer to it, retirement seems to loom, clearly visible on our horizon, much the same way a mountain range appears larger in your windshield as you drive across the flat landscape of the western United States. You may also liken conquering a peak to the efforts we put forth to save our money and accumulate enough resources to maintain in retirement a life-style equal to that which we enjoyed during our working years.

Camelback Mountain is 2,704 feet above sea level. That may not be impressive compared to other mountains like, say, Mount Hood in Oregon or Pike's Peak in Colorado, both of which are over 10,000 feet high. But no other city we know of boasts of its own mountain that competes with its skyscrapers for prominence and wins. The city of Phoenix provides trail maps for the 300,000 or so hikers that come each year to climb to the summit. Coincidentally, that's about how many people are turning 65 in America each year and coming to terms with the challenges of retirement. One of the reasons we decided to write this book is because the pathway to and through retirement is rife with pitfalls and hazards. Experience is a great teacher. Over the years, we have been sponges when it comes to gathering knowledge and education about successfully making the transition from working to retirement, and we feel that now it is time to become a spigot and pay it forward.

If you bought this book expecting to find a list of the 10 hottest stocks tips, or how to get in on the ground floor of the next Google, Apple or Microsoft, you will be disappointed (see us personally, and we will make arrangements for a refund). What you will find in these pages, however, are concepts and strategies that could help you avoid worrying that you will run out of money or lose your independence. Further, we are going to go out on a limb here and say categorically that there are no get-rich-quick schemes that work. What's that? You say you know someone who just won the lottery? Well, we would say that's an exception. Even then, the statistics on lottery winners whose money lasts longer than a few years just aren't that encouraging.

We do not know – and therefore cannot tell – the future. There, we've said it. It's out there for all to see, and we don't have to put a disclaimer at the end of the book. Precognition was not a course offered in the universities we attended. So you won't find many predictions and projections as you turn the pages of this book. What you will find, however, are ideas and financial solutions that work and are consistent with our times. The biggest fear among retirees is running out of money in old age. It's not the money so much as what the money represents to them – independence and self-determination. You will see examples of how just a little planning now can prevent such an outcome from becoming a real threat later.

Pensions used to be the mainstay of retirement income planning. Nowadays, they are all but extinct in America. Many who were on the verge of retiring and whose life's savings were in 401(k) accounts and mutual funds were shocked by the sudden losses they experienced during the 2008 stock market crash. Could something like that ever happen again? Not only could it happen again... it is likely to happen.

Some of the concepts and ideas you will read about here may be new to you. Don't let that throw you. Everything we have ever learned that proved valuable to us was new to us at one time. Keep an open mind and follow the logic we present along with the concepts and ideas. A teacher once asked, "If something you thought was true wasn't true, when would you want to know it?" If you are the type of person who responds, "As soon as possible!" then you will probably enjoy the rest of this book.

The views from the top of Camelback are downright amazing. On a clear day, the vista stretches for hundreds of miles. Some claim to have seen the lights of San Diego on a clear night. We believe that getting to the top of the mountain is good, but getting back down is even better. What in the world does that mean? We saw an interesting statistic recently on mountain climbing. Of all those who have died climbing Mount Everest, the majority by far, 85 percent in fact, died on the way back down. Think about that for a moment. You set out on a dangerous and difficult climb, and you make it to the top by hard work and staying focused on your goal. You celebrate for a while, take in the view, and then ready yourself for the trek back down the mountain. But things have changed. You are no longer looking upward toward the top of the mountain. Your focus has shifted, and you now see your goal from a different perspective. Everything has changed. Where is the adrenaline you had during the climb?

If you think of the mountain as your retirement, you save all your life to accumulate money to live on when you reach that "promised land." You have visions of taking life easy for a change. Enjoying long sunsets, traveling, playing on the beach with your grandchildren – whatever your vision of a carefree life after work may have been. You have finally made it to the day you have been looking forward to for so long. But this side of the timeline has new and unique challenges. Some of them may be the same challenges, only packaged differently. You are now in a position where it is vital to protect a nonrenewable income stream from inordinate market risk. Because you are older, there is greater potential for extended health care. Some challenges may be non-financial or psychological, such as the sorrow of losing a spouse or other close family member and coping both emotionally and financially with the aftermath. You may experience unexpected life circumstances such as having to care for aging parents or even adult children, or raising your grandchildren after a failed marriage.

For some, the realization hits them that what got them to retirement may not get them through retirement. You may have to reposition your assets to ensure that your income stream can last for the rest of your life. Whatever the case may be, the downhill side of the mountain can often be more unfriendly to you than the assent. Sometimes the stakes are higher, and the dangers more pronounced on the way back down. All of which explains why we say that getting to retirement is not the same as getting through retirement.

Finally, you will see that in this book we have nothing to sell, no agenda to promote, no axes to grind and no programs to push. All we wish to do is share with you the ideas and concepts that have allowed others to reach their financial goals. As we go about this, we will render certain truths about saving and investing. We will also candidly dispel certain myths and expose fatal fallacies that can threaten your retirement. Please understand, there is no malice in our candor. We just believe that clear thinking, full disclosure, accurate information and sound education are your best tools for climbing Retirement Mountain.

CHAPTER ONE

The Graying of the Baby Boom Generation

To qualify as a member of the baby boom generation, you have to have been born between 1946 and 1964. The term "baby boom" comes from the spike in the birth rate that occurred when American GIs returned from fighting World War II and settled down to civilian life.

No other generation changed American life as did the baby boom generation. They are still changing it. Have you noticed how many commercials these days are directed at senior citizens? There is a reason for that. Boomers have accumulated more wealth than any previous generation, and they are spending it on cars, homes, travel, goods and services.

At the start of World War II, the nation was still in the grip of the Great Depression. When the war ended in 1945, soldiers returned to an America that was experiencing an economic rebirth. Factories were producing again, and these new families were enthusiastic consumers of everything those factories could make. The boom generation was the driving force behind the emergence of the United States as the dominant world power and the cornerstone of the global economy. From the 1960s to the present day, boomers both made and consumed all that the nation's horn of plenty could produce – an endless stream of radios, televisions, cars, homes, appliances, computers, smartphones, and the list goes on.

To their credit (or perhaps discredit), baby boomers also invented the credit card. This handy little piece of plastic would satisfy their appetite for goods and services they wanted, but for which they could not afford to pay cash. "Buy now and pay later" became business as usual in the last half of the 20th century. The first credit card, introduced in 1950, was the Diners' Club card, and it was paper, not plastic. The Diners' Club was an actual club for people who wanted to dine at fine New York restaurants and have the restaurant bill their bank. Within just a few years, the banks allowed Diners' Club members to use the card at large department stores. Diners' Club soon became Master Charge (now MasterCard). Other bank cards emerged, such as Bank Americard (now Visa) and American Express.

Credit cards have proven to be both a convenience and a curse. Easy credit has been a trap for those boomers who have found it difficult to control their spending habits. There are more than 60 million credit card holders in America, and the average number of credit cards in the average boomer's wallet is seven. The average balance carried on each card is $2,500.

Journalist and author Tom Brokaw writes the following about the baby boom generation in his book, entitled "Boom":

"One minute it was Ike and the man in the gray flannel suit, and the next minute it was time to 'turn on, tune in, and drop out.' While Americans were walking on the moon, Americans were dying in Vietnam. Jackie Kennedy became Jackie O. There were tie dye shirts and hard hats, black power and law and order, Martin Luther King, Jr. and George Wallace, Ronald Reagan and Tom Hayden, Gloria Steinem and Anita Bryant, Mick Jagger and Wayne Newton. Well, you get the idea."

And Now They Are Retiring

According to the U.S. Census Bureau, the first member of the baby boom generation turned 65 on Jan. 1, 2011. At the time of this writing, there are 79 million baby boomers in America, which is about 10 times the population of New York City.

Every day approximately 10,000 baby boomers are severing themselves from their umbilical paychecks at work, making decisions on Medicare and Social Security, and preparing to enter a new phase of life – retirement. In this retirement stampede are some who have planned well for what lies ahead, but most have not. Some began thinking about their retirement well in advance. They identified how much they could expect from Social Security and how much of their retirement income would have to come from their personal resources. They diligently saved and invested wisely and are now poised to enjoy their "golden years" without worry.

Unfortunately, these folks are in the minority. Phillip Longman wrote a research paper entitled "Why Are So Many Baby Boomers Ill-Prepared for Retirement?" His research indicates that baby boomers earned more at every stage of life than any other generation in history, but, as a group, they didn't save enough of it. This generation had not had to pinch pennies just to have the necessities of life as did their parents. It was like the world was their oyster and pearls were just expected!

As a class, baby boomers have overspent and have failed to plan. If that isn't a recipe for bad times ahead, we don't know what is. To make it even worse, the Great Recession of 2008, as it is being called, wiped out a sizable portion of the savings of some of the ones who were already skating on thin ice with regard to their retirement savings. The Transamerica Center for Retirement Studies found that 54 percent of workers age 60 and above have not saved enough for retirement. The Employee Benefit Research

Institute reported that only 14 percent felt confident they would be able to live comfortably in retirement.

Pension? What Pension?

There was a time in America when you put in your 30 to 40 years at the office or factory you called your workaday home, and they gave you a gold watch and a nice pension. Between your pension and your Social Security, you were all set. But pensions are disappearing from the workplace now. If you have one, consider yourself one of the fortunate few. Defined-benefit plans began phasing out as defined-contribution plans such as the 401(k) began taking over in the 1990s. Big difference! Pension incomes were guaranteed for life. 401(k)s are typically invested in the stock market and, therefore, are subject to the possible losses that come along with the risk and volatility of the stock market. The events of 2008 put a big question mark on the viability of 401(k) plans as a reliable source of income in retirement.

To say that most boomers need help planning for retirement is a gross understatement. This generation, to which prosperity is seen almost as an entitlement, seems imbued with confidence that everything will turn out all right. Numbers, however, don't lie, and the math isn't looking all that great for millions of Americans who have no pension, inadequate savings, a shaky Social Security system, little or no understanding of the economy and sketchy plans for their financial future.

Living Longer May Present a Problem

Living longer is a good news/bad news situation. Wait a minute! What could possibly be bad about living longer? From the perspective of retirement income planning, the more years you will be alive in retirement, the more money you will need. The chances of running out of financial resources increase exponentially with each year you survive. Where does that money come from? While a longer life might be a bit of a good problem to have, it's a problem nonetheless.

A 2014 study by LIMRA Secure Retirement Institute found that having enough money to last throughout their lifetime is a top concern for retirees. A "worst case scenario" for many would be to outlive their resources and have to rely on the family members or the public dole for support. The study found that half of all pre-retiree and retiree U.S. households with assets of at least $100,000 are interested in converting assets into a guaranteed lifetime income for retirement.[1]

How long do you plan to live? It may interest you to know that, as a class, baby boomers on average are living longer than did their parents. It could be because of advancements in the field of medicine or better living habits (fewer smokers, more joggers, etc.), but the trend is definitely real. Just look at the statistics. In 1900, the average life expectancy in the United States was 47. By the time the 1960s rolled around it had risen to 69. In 2004, the average life expectancy was 80, and as this is written, it was 86.

The way life expectancy tables work, your attained age figures into the equation. In other words, if you live to the age of 70 you have a greater chance of living to 90. The number of centenarians (people aged 100 or more) is on the rise. The 1950 census recorded only 2,300 over the age of 100. The 2010 census recorded 53,364 Americans age 100 or older. Seniors outnumbered teenagers for the first time in history.

---

[1] Mark Morris, Catherine Theroux. Nov. 12, 2014. "LIMRA Secure Retirement Institute Survey Finds Interest in Guaranteed Retirement Income." http://www.limra.com/Posts/PR/News_Releases/LIMRA_Secure_Retirement_Institute _Survey_Finds_Interest_in_Guaranteed_Retirement_Income.aspx. Accessed Aug. 24, 2016.

Uniform Lifetime Table (partial)			
Age of IRA owner or plan participant	Life expectancy (in years)	Age of IRA owner or plan participant	Life expectancy (in years)
70	27.4	86	14.1
71	26.5	87	13.4
72	25.6	88	12.7
73	24.7	89	12.0
74	23.8	90	11.4
75	22.9	91	10.8
76	22.0	92	10.2
77	21.2	93	9.6
78	20.3	94	9.1
79	19.5	95	8.6
80	18.7	96	8.1
81	17.9	97	7.6
82	17.1	98	7.1
83	16.3	99	6.7
84	15.5	100	6.3
85	14.8	101	5.9

Source: Strategy Financial Group

We have noticed a trend in our conversations with clients who are near or in retirement about their income planning. More of them are interested in lifetime guarantees. They seem to want assurances – not projections – when it comes to their future income.

Baby Boomers

Demographics

- The number of baby boomers in the United States is 79 million. This is nearly 10 times the current population of New York City.
- Between now and 2029, U.S. baby boomers will turn age 65 at a rate of roughly 10,000 per day.
- 7 in 10 of today's 65-year-old females are expected to live until at least age 80; more than 1/3 are expected to live to at least age 90; the corresponding figures for men are 6 in 10 to age 80 and nearly one quarter to age 90. (Source: Society of actuaries; Insured Retirement Institute)

Retirement Planning

- Nearly 1/2 of baby boomers are at risk for having inadequate retirement income.
- Nearly 1/4 of baby boomers have not saved for retirement; and 46% have not tried to determine the amount they need to save.
- 27 percent of baby boomers expect to work at least part-time during retirement; 8% have adopted a "work until you drop" attitude, indicating that they do not plan to retire.
- Marital status is a factor in retirement income planning; just 2 out of 10 unmarried women believe they are doing a good job of preparing for their retirement years, compared to 4 out of 10 married women.

(Source: Employee Benefit Research Institute)

Investment Advice Tsunami

Have you noticed how many experts there are these days offering investment advice? On cable TV, there are as many finance channels as there are sports channels. The magazine rack at the bookstore is overflowing with magazines on investing. Just type the words "financial advice" in the Google search bar and millions of sites pop up. Hang around the water cooler at the office, and you are bound to pick up a hot stock tip. The next door neighbor wants to let you in on what his broker swears is a ground floor opportunity. When it comes to financial advice, we don't have to go looking for it. We are awash in it, and it seems to come from every corner.

It would be nice, of course, if we could just click on the TV, flip to the finance channels and draft a financial plan based on what the talking heads tell us. Wouldn't it be great if we could pluck a $2.50 magazine off the rack, read the article, follow the advice therein, and by so doing carve out a secure financial future for ourselves? And how convenient it would be for us if good old Uncle Fred really did know what the next Apple or Google stock was, and we could buy into it when it was still at $10 per share. But those are pipe dreams. The truth is, there is no silver bullet, no magic beans and no easy, get-rich-quick scheme that works.

The headlines on the magazines compete for your attention:

"Five Stocks You MUST buy NOW!"

"Why You Should Invest In GOLD This Year"

"Top 10 Hot Stock Tips"

Have you noticed that there are never headlines recommending the slow and steady approach to investing? Why? There is nothing exciting about that. It also makes for better television when two "experts" duel it out on a split screen, each having polar opposite views on the same topic. The truth is probably somewhere in the middle, and slow and steady investing usually wins the race.

It's no wonder that some people, confounded by the conflicting advice, just throw their hands up in frustration and decide not to decide. But that's not an acceptable option either, since failure to plan is planning to fail. So whom can we trust and where can we go to get solid and objective financial counseling?

CHAPTER TWO

Anything Can Happen at Any Time

Planning for the future would be a breeze if it weren't for the fact that life is full of surprises, and anything can happen at any time to throw a kink in the works. Since we can't know the future, the next best thing is to be as prepared as possible for unexpected events *before they occur.*

We tell our younger clients that one of their first priorities should be setting up an emergency fund for unexpected life events that can place a sudden strain on one's cash supply. Such things as losing a job, a sudden illness or injury, or even a car breaking down can put your financial house in disarray. How much should an emergency fund contain? We recommend you keep at least six months' worth of living expenses in the bank. Nine months is better, of course. Also, to qualify as an "emergency fund" it should be kept in an account that is liquid and safe from risk.

Older Americans are more vulnerable to life's unexpected events than are younger people. By the time you have worked (and hopefully saved) for a few decades, there is more at stake. A poor decision could wipe out years of diligent saving and investing. This happened to millions of Americans in 2008.

Expect the Unexpected

The Titanic was a modern marvel of construction. When it launched in 1912, it was the largest and most luxurious passenger vessel of its time. Because it had eight watertight compartments that would automatically close if the hull was breached, the ship was thought to be unsinkable.

> "I cannot imagine any condition which would cause a ship to founder. I cannot conceive of any vital disaster happening to this vessel. Modern shipbuilding has gone beyond that."
> ~ *Captain E.J. Smith of the Titanic, speaking of Titanic's older sister, the Adriatic*
>
> "Overconfidence seems to have dulled the faculties usually so alert."
> ~ *Sen. William Smith, on Captain E.J. Smith.*

When the Titanic left on her maiden voyage from the port city of Southampton on the southern coast of England, the mood was festive. The 2,224 passengers aboard included some of the wealthiest people in the world. No one paid attention to the details, such as:

- The ship carried only 20 lifeboats.
- The capacity of each lifeboat was 65 or fewer.
- Icebergs had been spotted in the North Atlantic along the ship's intended route to New York.

Four days into the crossing and about 375 miles south of Newfoundland, Titanic struck an iceberg, the glancing collision slicing open too much of the ship's hull for the watertight compartments to save her. Two hours later, she broke apart and sank with over 1,000 people still aboard. Only 705 people survived. Years later, it would be said that it wasn't an iceberg that sank the Titanic so much as it was overconfidence.

On Sept. 29, 2008, the Dow Jones Industrial Average dropped 777 points. It was the largest one-day drop in the history of the stock market. Millions of Americans who had money invested in stocks, mutual funds and retirement accounts lost trillions of dollars. It was the sinking of the good ship Wall Street. I remember watching the news that night on TV. The nation was shocked and amazed that such a sell-off could happen. Hadn't safeguards been put in place to prevent this kind of thing?

Dow Jones Industrial Average Historical Returns

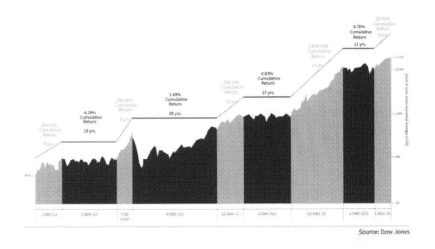

Source: Dow Jones

In the case of the Titanic, the tragedy occurred on a night when there was not a ripple on the ocean. It was smooth sailing all the way. It was the same with the economy in the years leading up to the 2008 crash. The investing public felt like the "tech bubble," or the "dot com bust" that caused the 2000 meltdown had just been a bump in the road, and now the Wall Street juggernaut had returned to the glory days of the 1990s, a time when stock charts knew only one direction – up! But there were warning signs. The Dow had started off 2007 at 12,459 and was racing forward with a head of steam provided by what some warned was a "housing bubble." Like the warnings of icebergs in the North Atlantic, the warnings that the housing bubble was near bursting were drowned out by the staccato sound of hammers putting up condominiums and subdivisions all across the country and the roar of the money waterfall that was funding it all. Construction loans were flowing like water. Homebuyers were scrambling to get in on the land rush. Many were buying on speculation in an easy-money atmosphere that had been created by the megabanks.

At the bottom of the food chain, all that was required to obtain a loan was a promise to make the payments. What did the banks care? If you defaulted on the loan, they would take over your property, which was bound to increase in value with each passing year. The icebergs of that day and time were exotic loans such as the "No-Doc NINA," which stood for "no documentation, no income and no assets," and interest-only loans, which allowed the borrower to pay only the interest and none of the principal with each payment. Both those loans are rare if not extinct as this is written. Adjustable rate mortgage loans (ARMs) were popular during the housing boom. Many of these loans were obtained by homebuyers who focused only on the monthly mortgage payment. No problem if the payment went up in a few years. By that time, the value of the property would surely be higher, and they could refinance. When home values fell precipitously after 2008, those chickens came home, as they say, to roost.

Just as some were worried about the ice field into which the Titanic steamed, there were some in government who worried about the direction in which the economy was heading in 2007. By August of that year, the Federal Reserve began to see that some of the too-big-to-fail banks were experiencing a liquidity problem. The Fed began to take measures to shore them up, essentially pumping money into the system.[2] This was proof to some observers that the economy had entered the "danger zone."

The Economy Collides With Derivatives

In the summer of 2007, word began to leak out about the trouble the megabanks were having. Before then, few outside the banking world knew what a derivative was. News reporters, trying to get to the bottom of things, made "derivatives" a virtual household word. As the word suggests, a derivative is something that is derived or based upon, something else. In bank-speak, a derivative is a financial instrument that derives its value from an underlying asset, index or interest rate. In and of themselves, derivatives have no actual value. Their only value is that which is placed in them by those who deem them to be worth something.

See how murky that is? See where this was all heading? Government auditors dug deeper and deeper until it finally became apparent that the collateral for the billions and billions of dollars in loans the megabanks had made to wholesale banks, who in turn made loans to the end users, was (drum roll please) ... *derivatives.* The housing bubble was a self-inflating balloon kept in the air by bad loans.

Warren Buffett, in the 2002 Berkshire Hathaway annual report, had the following to say about derivatives:

> "I view derivatives as time bombs, both for the parties that deal in them and the economic system. Basically these instruments call for money to change hands at some future date, with the amount to be determined by one or more reference items, such as interest rates, stock prices or currency values. Central banks and governments have so far found no effective way to control, or even monitor, the risks posed by these contracts. ... In my

---

[2] Board of Governors of the Federal Reserve System. July 27, 2016. "Monetary Policy." http://www.federalreserve.gov/monetarypolicy/. Accessed Aug. 24, 2016.

view, derivatives are financial weapons of mass destruction, carrying dangers that, while now latent, are potentially lethal."

In hindsight, Buffet's words were nothing short of prophetic. When the government decided to bail out the too-big-to-fail banks, Uncle Sam was essentially accepting subprime mortgages, the root of the problem, as collateral. The list of big banks that fell as a result of the subprime mortgage crisis in the spring and summer of 2008 included such venerable lending entities as Bear Stearns and the twin towers of Fannie Mae (Federal National Mortgage Association) and Freddie Mac (Federal Home Loan Mortgage Corporation). In September, Lehman Brothers declared bankruptcy followed by the American International Group (AIG), which has run out of cash attempting to cover the credit default swaps it had issued against mortgage-backed securities. Investors watched helplessly as the Dow lost hundreds of points on a daily basis, culminating in the record-setting 777.68-point loss suffered on Sept. 29, 2008. Doom and gloom had settled like a blanket over Wall Street, and the Great Recession of 2008 was underway.

Retirees and those approaching retirement were hurt the most because of where they were in the stream of time.

"Retirement Savings Lose $2 Trillion in 15 Months," read a headline in the Washington Post on Oct. 8, 2008.

"Retirement Accounts Have Now Lost $3.4 Trillion," blared another in the U.S. News and World Report, March 13, 2009.

The Human Side of Financial Loss

Through the public retirement workshops we conduct, we came into close contact with many who lost as much as half of their life's savings in the 2008 market decline. Even now from time to time, we find ourselves in front of a somber audience comprising more than one individual who was affected by that dark Monday when the market lost $1.2 trillion in a single day.[3] Although we may have a topic that we intend to cover, such as income laddering techniques, the discussion is sometimes taken over by those still reeling from the hits they have taken in the past decade from Wall Street.

At that point, we must abandon our agenda for the meeting and open it up to questions; there are plenty of them.

"Why didn't my broker see this coming?"

"Is the market going to go any lower?"

"When will it turn around?"

"What should we do? Stay in or get out?

"Don't we have people in Washington that are supposed to prevent this sort of thing from happening?" asked one frustrated man.

One couple who came into our office for a consultation told us they had lost nearly 40 percent of their life savings in the 2008 market freefall.

"We just weren't paying attention," the husband said, explaining that they had always trusted someone else to manage their money.

They were businesspeople. They owned and ran a combination convenience store/car wash and self-service laundry. As they put it: "We were too busy making the money to worry about managing it. We didn't have enough time to pay attention to what was happening on Wall Street. But why didn't someone tell us that a thing like this could happen? We would have moved our money to somewhere safe."

The answer, of course, was that no one has a crystal ball. The stock market is unpredictable. No matter how much experience

---

[3] Alexandra Twin. CNNMoney. Sept. 29, 2008. "Stocks crushed." http://money.cnn.com/2008/09/29/markets/markets_newyork/. Accessed Aug. 24, 2016.

any financial professional possesses, and regardless of how many letters follow his or her name on a business card, that individual, unless blessed with supernatural abilities of precognition, does not know what will happen tomorrow. Yet looking at the way this couple's plans for their impending retirement had been altered by the unexpected turn of events on Wall Street, we could understand how they felt. They felt betrayed. From their perspective, it was like going to a medical professional for advice and being misdiagnosed, or paying an accountant to handle your taxes and then getting a letter from the IRS accusing you of tax evasion. In their minds, their broker had fumbled the ball.

"We had it all figured out," the woman said. "We had six months to go before we retired. We were going to sell the business to our son-in-law and buy a small motor home. We were going to take a year or two and just travel to all the places we always wanted to see and take our time doing it. Maybe visit some friends and relatives along the way. Then we figured that, between our Social Security and what we had in our retirement account, we would have enough to live comfortably the rest of our lives."

"Most of that went down the tubes," said the man. "We are only just now getting back to where we might retire."

A Huge Responsibility

When the Titanic sank, the captain went down with the ship in the finest British tradition. The most reliable reports are that he locked himself in the cabin 10 minutes before the water finally washed over the bridge and that he sank with the doomed vessel, stoically holding onto the ship's useless wheel.

We feel that advising clients on how to handle their money is a huge responsibility, especially when they are nearing the junction of life when they are jettisoning the regular paycheck and must now rely on other resources, some of them finite and nonrenewable, for support. While it may be true that the broker who advised the couple mentioned before could not have known that a market crash would occur just as they were getting ready to retire, that doesn't relieve him from some of the responsibility for what happened. Competent financial advisers should understand the behavior of the stock market. That is what they are there for. They know that along with the potential for gains in the stock market comes the risk of loss, and that the closer to retirement a client is, the more of his or her assets should be placed in conservative investments. Retirement is not the time to be pushing all your chips to the center of the table, as it were, and, to use a poker term, "go all in," with a portfolio solely invested in an unpredictable stock market.

In the case of this couple, they were in their early-to-mid-60s. Their savings were almost completely in market-based mutual funds, which were 100 percent at risk. The responses they heard from those into whose hands they had entrusted their financial future all had the same ring to it. "You're not alone: everybody lost money in this one," and "Just stay put, it will come back." Those responses are accurate on both counts. Problem was, this couple didn't have "eventually" to wait. They were left deciding how much longer they would have to postpone their retirement to allow them time to build their savings back up.

It is impossible to unring a bell. And there is a colloquial farming expression that says something about locking the barn door after the cow has escaped. The task ahead of us with this couple, however, was to help them pick up the pieces and get a fresh start. We hammered out a strategy that would enable them to regain as much as possible of what they had lost without risking what they still possessed. Their new financial house would be stronger all around. But there was no getting around the fact that they would have to continue working a few more years. With this couple, we were clear in our counsel to them that one of the **worst** things to do after a major loss in your retirement account is to "double down," as they say in Las Vegas, and go back to the same roulette wheel that robbed you in an attempt to get it back. There is one footnote to this episode that we need to include, and, as true as it is, we did not express it to them – at least not in these blunt terms – because we felt they were already painfully aware of it by the time our initial planning sessions were complete: *You must take responsibility for your own financial future.* That doesn't mean that you shouldn't seek professional help. In fact, we recommend it. But placing your trust in a financial adviser who is not a fiduciary and not legally obligated to give you directions that are in your best interests is a mistake few approaching retirement can afford to make. We will elaborate on this theme later on in this book. But you are the only one who can decide whether the financial help you select and the financial advice you act upon will put you safely where you want to be in retirement, or leave you on thin ice, wondering what went wrong.

CHAPTER THREE

Protecting Your Nest Egg From Predators

'When you ain't got nothin'
You got nothin' to lose"
~Bob Dylan, 'Like a Rolling Stone"

We hear the term "nest egg" a lot in our line of work. It is the word people use to describe the money they have salted away for retirement. It is an apt term because it signifies something fragile and precious. You have worked hard all your life, and you have saved diligently, sometimes even sacrificing to have your reserve. It would be a shame, after all this time and effort, to lose it. It is appropriate that we strive to protect our "nest egg." Safeguard it from danger.

In nature, robins will make their nests in all kinds of crazy places in an attempt to prevent squirrels, blue jays and other predatory birds from attacking them. Robins' nests have been found in construction cranes, moving railroad cars, even under the hoods of junk cars. These small birds will fight ferociously to protect their young, taking on birds three times their size.

As we edge closer to retirement, it is prudent to be alert for predators.

A study conducted by MetLife found older Americans lose nearly $3 billion per year to financial abuse. Half of it is perpetrated by strangers. Sadly, 34 percent of this abuse is at the hands of relatives and family friends. Exploitation by the business sector accounts for the remaining 16 percent. Women are twice as likely to be victims of elder financial abuse as men, according to the study.

A 70-year-old client called into our offices the other day and excitedly told us that she had just won $680,000. "Could it possibly be a scam?" she asked, understandably hoping it wasn't.

Hers is not an isolated case. She is one of the hundreds of thousands who are targeted each year by con artists whose goal is to separate trusting and unsuspecting senior citizens from their money. This scam began when the woman received an email from a bogus law firm informing her that she was the winner of a sweepstakes. The email said this was the law firm's final attempt to reach her. We doubted very much that there had been any other attempts to reach her before this, but she had been in the hospital recently, so the idea that they had tried and failed to contact her seemed plausible to her.

When we began to dissect the wording in the email, looking for the catch, as we suspected, the firm didn't exist. We searched the internet using every possible combination we could think of, and there was no listing of any such law firm. The email had come from a Yahoo! account that could have been set up by anyone using false information. The instructions the email contained were clear, however. She was told that before she could collect her lottery winnings, she must immediately wire the exact sum of $2,870 to the law firm to cover insurance costs. Once this was done, they would send out her $680,000. We informed the police about the scam, of course, but the perpetrators of this fraud were untraceable, as most of them are.

Other Frauds and Scams

The Financial Industry Regulatory Authority, or FINRA, reported on Sept. 12, 2013, that in one of their surveys, 80 percent of respondents said they had received a "potentially fraudulent offer," and 11 percent reported having lost "a significant amount of money" by falling for a scam.

We read where one senior citizen in South Florida lost $9,500 when she was told that she needed to pay that amount in taxes first in order to claim a $1 million sweepstakes prize. These are typical of "pay-to-receive-your-prize" rip-offs, according to the Federal Trade Commission, which collects thousands of such reports each year.

Sometimes the callers say they are representing a government agency and are so bold as to ask for Social Security numbers, credit card numbers, bank information and passwords. One of the latest of these takes advantage of the naivety surrounding the Affordable Care Act (Obamacare). You are told that you need a new Medicare card to keep from losing coverage. To process this card, they need access to your bank accounts.

By now, most people have heard of the so-called "Nigerian scam." This is where someone claiming to be a deposed prince from Nigeria says he has millions of dollars and wants to transfer it all to you. All he needs is your bank account information. There are many versions of this ruse, always with emails that open with "Hello kind stranger," or words to that effect.

If there is one thing we have learned through helping people with their problems over the years, it is that anything that **sounds** too good to be true is probably **not** true. You can put that little truism right up there with "Where there is smoke, there's fire," and "Don't take any wooden nickels." The best way to protect yourself is to reject out of hand the idea that anything worthwhile is free or easy to obtain or that you are somehow lucky. Sure, you may occasionally be lucky. And sure, something of value may fall into your lap at some point in your life. But having a healthy skepticism about such occurrences will prevent you from being taken in.

The Biggest Ponzi Scheme Ever

Everybody by now has heard of Bernie Madoff. His name has become synonymous with financial fraud the way the name Boris Karloff became synonymous with vampire movies. Madoff's name wouldn't live in infamy had it not been for the inclination of those he duped to believe in something that was too good to be true. In 2008, when every other brokerage firm in the nation was showing losses, Madoff's accounts continued to earn healthy interest. You would think that would have been a major tipoff that something was wrong. The problem was, his victims *wanted* to believe the unbelievable. Even in the face of evidence to the contrary, most of his account holders held on, smugly imagining that they had outsmarted the system. The phrase "Ponzi scheme" appeared in several headlines explaining the $50 billion ruse that Madoff played on his victims. The scheme was named after an Italian con man named Charles Ponzi, who became infamous in the early 1920s by promising clients unreasonably high returns over a short period. He perfected the game of using paying early investors "returns" on the backs of later investors, who would, of course, be left holding the bag when he ran out of "customers."

Madoff, who makes Ponzi look like a street pickpocket, pleaded guilty in 2009 and is now identified as inmate No. 61727-054 at

Butner Federal Correction Complex where, as we write this, he is serving a 150-year prison sentence.[4]

The Promissory Note Scheme

One couple we know of had lived frugally all of their lives. They had grown up in the Great Depression and understood the value of money. They were careful not to waste anything. In their modest home, they believed in turning off the lights when leaving a room. They seldom ate in restaurants, and when they did, they nearly always carried any leftovers home in "doggie bags" to save in the refrigerator for later. Even though they would admit to having "a few thousand in the bank," it was more like a few hundred thousand.

One afternoon when they were in their late 70s, an insurance agent visited them because a mutual friend had mentioned their name as being worthy of a special opportunity. The agent represented what appeared to be a legitimate company. He was friendly and charming. They saw nothing in his manner that would indicate he was out to take advantage of them. And he wasn't – not consciously, anyway. But they were about to be the next victims of the "promissory note scam."

The ones who work this scheme stay in the shadows. They don't approach the victims personally. In fact, there are two layers of deceit involved in this one: (a) an insurance agent who is promised high commissions and agrees to work for what he thinks is a legitimate company, and (b) the naïve investor who wants a better-than-average return.

---

[4] The Associated Press. July 14, 2009. "Call him prisoner No. 61727-054: Bernie Madoff enters N.C. federal prison to begin 150-year sentence."http://www.nydailynews.com/news/money/call-prisoner-no-61727-054-bernie-madoff-enters-n-federal-prison-150-year-sentence-article-1.394145. Accessed Aug. 24, 2016.

The insurance agent is supplied with sales materials that look legitimate, but the information on them is bogus. A legitimate promissory note is sometimes used by large companies to raise money through loans. They are sometimes used business to business. The investor company loans money to a start-up company in return for the promise of repayment with interest at the end of a specified period. But promissory notes are not usually sold to the general public. This couple didn't know that. The promissory note document was printed on quality paper. It looked quite official. Neither the couple nor the insurance agent knew that the issuing company was fictitious. The hook was the promise of a 15 percent return within a year. This didn't seem suspicious to the older couple. They remembered the high-inflation days of the late 1970s and early 1980s when interest rates on bank CDs had been that high. Perhaps it was a return to "the good old days," when they actually got something in return for their money. The couple sunk $100,000 into the program, approximately one-fourth of their life savings.

When there was no interest check at the end of the first year of their contract, they began trying to contact the issuing firm, only to find out that there was no such firm and that the telephone numbers they had been given were no longer in service. The con artists used a portion of the $100,000 to pay the insurance agent, but the rest was in the wind. After the matter was turned over to the authorities, the insurance agent was as distraught as the couple. He lost his license, but he couldn't pay the couple back. The perpetrators of the scam had taken advantage of dozens of others before leaving town, leaving no trail for investigators.

It Pays to Be Cautious

After the Madoff scandal, Washington put more regulations in place to prevent such chicanery, but scam artists don't care. They have never played by the rules anyway. The best defense is an attitude of watchfulness for any opportunity that sounds too good to be true.

As mentioned earlier in this book, you are ultimately responsible for your own financial future. No one else. You. Does that mean that you shouldn't seek the help of a professional financial adviser for assistance? Of course not! No more than you would practice self-surgery or fail to seek medical attention just because there are quacks out there, or because there is the possibility of receiving bad advice. But you should do your due diligence and select an adviser who is a fiduciary and legally bound to put your interests ahead of his or her own. It is prudent to protect your wealth the same way you would protect your health. In subsequent chapters, we will explore specific questions – a checklist, if you will – that will help you in your quest to choose the adviser that has the knowledge, the skillset and the legal obligation to help you climb your retirement peak and make your descent without endangering the nest egg you have saved for retirement.

CHAPTER FOUR

Beware of Phantom Income

Phantom—pronounced \ fan-təm\ – the soul of a dead person thought of as living in an unseen world or as appearing to living people. Something illusionary, something that is not real and exists only in a persons mind."~ Merriam-Webster Dictionary

In the jargon of the financial world, **phantom income** is reportable income that you don't actually receive. It could be income from investments such as stocks or bonds or mutual funds or even income-producing real estate or bank CDs. If those accounts produce interest, dividends or gains, you get hit with taxes on the earnings even if you never use the money to live on, or invest for a rainy day. Even if your account lost value on paper, you wind up paying income tax if the account has phantom income.

For example, phantom income is associated with zero-coupon bonds. Traditional bonds are pretty straightforward. They pay annual interest that is usually taxed. But with zero-coupon bonds, no interest is paid. The bondholder is still presented with a statement of what is called "imputed" interest. The amount of imputed interest with which you are credited is based on the eventual realized gain, broken down over the life of the bond. This imputed interest is taxed each year, just like interest from a traditional bond. The drawback of a zero-coupon bond is that you have to pay taxes on the price appreciation of the bond while you are holding it, even though you don't have control over the income. The way zero-coupon bonds work, they are issued at a discount and mature at "par value," another way of saying face value, or value at maturity. The bondholder effectively receives the payments when the bond matures at the higher value. Interest payments, however, are credited to the bondholder for tax purposes even though no check is actually cut.

Loan forgiveness is another form of phantom income. The creditor essentially "pays" the delinquent borrower the amount of debt forgiven, which is why creditors send IRS Form 1099-C to the borrower showing the amount of "income" that he or she received as forgiven debt. For obvious reasons, phantom income is something most taxpayers generally tend to eschew if at all possible. Phantom income is unavoidable in some cases, but in others, it can be avoided with just a little planning.

Phantom Income and Taxes on Social Security

Phantom income can cause you to pay unnecessary taxes on your Social Security. We call this the "senior-only tax" because, with a few exceptions, only senior citizens collect Social Security benefits. Is it fair that you should have to pay any income tax on Social Security? Weren't you taxed on the money that went into the program? Well, fair or not, the law is the law.

- If your combined income is under $25,000 for singles ($32,000 for couples filing jointly), then your Social Security benefits aren't taxable.
- If your combined income is between $25,000 and $34,000 for singles ($32,000 to $44,000 for couples), then you will have to pay income tax on up to 50 percent of your benefit.

- If your combined income is over $34,000 for singles ($44,000 for couples), then you will have to pay income tax on up to 85 percent of your benefit.

The "Senior Only" Tax

In this world of extreme tolerance and ultra-sensitivity to political correctness, it is hard to believe that there exists such a discriminatory tax that is considered unfair by millions of Americans, and they don't think there is anything they can do about it. But there is. We are talking, of course, about income taxes on Social Security benefits.

Have you ever heard of the "Golden Promise?" Folklore has it that when Franklin Delano Roosevelt signed the Social Security Act into law in 1935, a reporter shouted out the question, "Mr. Roosevelt, Mr. Roosevelt ... are you going to tax Social Security benefits?"

The story goes that the president pounded his fist on the desk in the Oval Office and bellowed, "I will NEVER tax Social Security!"

The Social Security Administration says that never happened and FDR never uttered those words. The SSA Office of Public Inquires acknowledges that Social Security benefits were not originally considered taxable income, but they maintain that it was never a provision of the law that they not be taxed. Historians can't find any record to support FDR's oath either. Even if he did say it, it's a moot point now. FDR died in 1945; Social Security benefits remained untaxed as long as he was alive.

In 1982, it became apparent that the Social Security system was going broke. President Ronald Reagan appointed a committee, led by Alan Greenspan, to fix it. When they met, word got out that Social Security cuts were on their way. The AARP organized a march to protest. A group calling themselves the "Gray Panthers," led by senior activist Maggie Kuhn, paraded before the TV cameras carrying signs that urged "No Social Security Cuts!" It was quite a show.

That meeting spawned the Social Security Amendments of 1983, which would forever impose a tax beginning in 1984. The way the new law was worded, if you were a single taxpayer and your base annual income was $25,000 or more, or if you were a married couple filing jointly and your base annual income was $32,000 or more, then up to 50 percent of your Social Security check would be treated as taxable income.

That held until 1993, when President Bill Clinton raised taxation to 85 percent of benefits for single beneficiaries with incomes over $34,000 and couples over $44,000.

The Key Word Is "Reportable"

Is there anything that can be done about this "senior-only" tax? Yes. Keep in mind, Uncle Sam giveth with one hand and taketh away with the other. One of the questions we like to ask our audiences at the educational workshops we conduct is: "Who do you think pays more in taxes ... the informed or the uninformed?"

The envelope, please. Answer: The uninformed.

Before we go any further, let us say that, if you are like most loyal, patriotic American citizens, you may grumble a little, but you don't mind paying your fair share of taxes – you just don't want to pay more than your fair share. Tax avoidance is not tax evasion. There's an old joke that goes something like this: "What's the difference between tax *evasion* and tax *avoidance?*"

"Oh, about 10-20 years."

The tax avoidance strategies we are talking about are printed by the government for all to see. They are right there in the IRS code. The only problem is, the Internal Revenue Code is 7,500 pages long and contains 3.4 million words. You just have to know where to look. Competent financial advisers know where to look.

We have seen some instances where a couple may have a bank CD that pays them $500 in annual interest – and it is just enough to kick them over into the taxable bracket, even if they leave the money in the CD. Dividends from brokerage accounts can do the same thing, even if you reinvest the earnings back into the account. Most taxpayers just accept this as a matter of course and think there is nothing they can do about it. Tax preparers, especially the ones who merely fill in the boxes, aren't aware of any way around it either. Each situation is unique, of course, but in many cases, there are legitimate, perfectly legal and ethical ways to avoid paying this tax.

Reportable vs. Non-Reportable Income

Look at Line 20A of your IRS Form1040 where you record your income for Social Security, and Line 20B where you see the amount of your Social Security income that is subject to taxation. What we want to do, if we can, is keep Line 20B blank by controlling the reportable income from other sources. The IRS makes a distinction between reportable and non-reportable income. The key is to reposition some of your assets into accounts where the income generated is either tax deferred or tax free.

You can buy United States Savings Bonds. You know the ones we're talking about – you buy them for $25, and if you keep them long enough they mature to $50. You never pay taxes on that money until you actually take the money out.

You can also move your money into tax-deferred annuities. Annuities are issued by insurance companies. They are safe investments. Fixed annuities pay a guaranteed interest rate, typically a little higher than what banks pay. A difference between income from a fixed annuity and a bank CD is that you don't pay any income tax on the money as it's earned – only when you actually draw it out. Fixed index annuities are also tax-deferred. They do not have a fixed interest rate. They go up to a certain point as the market goes up. But when the market goes down, they stay up. We will discuss these in greater detail in subsequent chapters of this book, but the point is, by moving income producing assets from reportable to non-reportable accounts, you may reduce or even eliminate unnecessary taxation on Social Security.

Three Bucket System

One way to take control is to use what we call "three-bucket planning." Most uninformed retirees use a single bucket for their investments, where everything is taxable. Our suggestion is to take better control of page one of our tax return. The informed retiree is at least using two-bucket planning – one bucket for current needs where the income is taxable and another bucket of tax-deferred income for non-current needs. If we don't need the income, put it in a tax-deferred bucket and tap into it only when you need it. The more money you keep growing in a tax-deferred status, the quicker it can compound.

What's bucket three? That's for money you don't think you will use in your lifetime. It's money you have mentally set aside as a legacy for your kids and grandkids. Keep this money tax-exempt – not only for income tax but also for estate planning purposes. For example, some have assets they do not intend to use. They fully intend to pass them along to their heirs when they die. Yet, they maintain these assets in a brokerage account or in bank CDs where they must pay annual taxes on the gains and where the assets are fully exposed to estate taxes when inherited. Why not place these assets in a tax-exempt bucket for your spouse or the next generation? Then they would be tax exempt not only for income tax but estate planning purposes, too. That's what well-informed retirees are doing. How? Read on.

Eliminating the Tax Bite

So your investment at Big Brokerage is earning 6 percent, and you are feeling pretty good about that. Let's see ... 6 percent minus 33 percent in taxes = 4 percent. That's what we call "money falling through the cracks." Why don't the people at Big Brokerage Company talk much about taxes when you go there? Because taxes aren't on their radar. If you ask what most people pay in taxes, you will likely get an answer of around 10 percent, which doesn't sound too bad, right? But hold on a second. We can't just look at the tax rate; we have to look at the marginal tax rate. That's the rate at which your investment will be taxed. That's going to be anywhere from 18 percent to 33 percent. One-third of every investment you own is going down the drain in taxes. Why not put as much of the income you are not actually using in a tax-deferred bucket?

Now, keep in mind that tax deferral is not tax elimination. Deferring your taxes means you will have to pay Uncle Sam on that money eventually. This means that, to avoid over-taxation at a later date, you will want to be prepared with a withdrawal strategy, keeping an eye on your marginal tax rate.

Another investment strategy to consider is the possibility of saving money in (or perhaps even converting funds to) a Roth IRA. Like traditional IRAs, Roths are long-term retirement accounts. Unlike traditional IRAs, however, your contributions to a Roth account are taxed at your current income tax rate, so they will not be taxed later. Particularly if you think taxes are likely to increase, and if you think you may be in the same tax bracket in retirement as during your working years, Roth IRAs should be on your list of considerations.

Roth IRA Contributions Quick Facts[5]

- Can be set up at your job
- You contribute already-taxed funds (after-tax funds) to a Roth
- You receive no tax deductions for your Roth contributions
- You can continue to contribute after age 70 ½
- Qualified withdrawals are income tax free (qualified withdrawals are made by an over-59-½ account owner from a Roth that has been established for more than 5 years OR are made by the owner as a first-time homebuyer OR are made after the owner has died or is disabled)
- You can contribute to a spousal Roth IRA, based on your income, even if your spouse has no personal income
- You may convert a traditional IRA to a Roth. To do so, you must pay current income taxes on and leave your converted monies in the Roth account for 5 years and avoid making withdrawals until you have reached age 59 ½
- Similar to traditional IRAs, unqualified withdrawals from a Roth IRA could result in a 10% tax penalty
- A Roth IRA's designated beneficiaries can stretch distributions over their lifetimes the same as traditional IRA beneficiaries
- Unlike traditional IRAs, account owners do not have government-required minimum withdrawals

As you can see, there are more than a few reasons why Roth IRAs are attractive to those who are looking to put more in their tax-free asset bucket.

---

[5] Ed Slott and Company LLC. 2015. "Roth IRA Contributions Quick Fact Sheet." https://www.irahelp.com/printable/roth-ira-contributions-quick-fact-sheet. Accessed Dec. 6, 2016.

Phantom Income Tax

Let's say a few years back you sat down with your financial adviser or broker, and you invested $500,000 in a mutual fund. And now, five years later, that account has a value of $425,000. You take your statement down to the broker, and you say, "I'm a little confused. We gave you $500,000 from our nest egg several years ago. We haven't taken any distributions, and it's now worth only $425,000."

"It's OK," says the broker. "It's only a loss on **paper.**"

Then January rolls around, and you open up your mailbox and there staring back at you is a 1099 tax form with a distribution of $15,000. You take the 1099 tax form to your CPA and ask the accountant, "What is this $15,000 distribution?"

Now your tax adviser has to explain to you that, during the year, the mutual fund manager, when they were selling off stocks, sold off stocks at a gain. Although the sum of the funds in your mutual fund has decreased, one of the shares was sold at a gain, called a capital gain. By federal law, that gain must be taxed.

"But I never got a check in the mail," you protest.

"I understand that," says the accountant, "but there's a little bit of good news. The income tax rate on that distribution is at an all-time low – 15 percent!"

Irony of ironies, you sit in front of your accountant and have to write a check to Uncle Sam for $2,250 on an account that lost value and cranked out a distribution you never saw. And in the years that Wall Street goes downward or sideways, sometimes many years in a row, this tax in this example could be $10,000 or $11,000. Your account has locked in that capital gain, true, but it can be frustrating that the oft-repeated platitude of "paper losses" doesn't seem to ring true when it comes to "paper gains."

Plugging the Leaks

Competent financial advisers are like plumbers. They find "money leaks" and fix them. You worked hard and saved diligently. What a shame to lose one "drop" of your assets to the taxman unnecessarily. Finding the phantom income that can cause unfair taxation is a major part of an adviser's job. Using deferral strategies such as the ones mentioned above keeps your money in your wallet and in your family

Hidden Fees

Another area of financial management where you have to watch your back is hidden fees in mutual funds. You would like to think that the people operating these investments would be an open book and engage in full disclosure, but such is apparently not the case. Mutual funds have been nailed in the financial press in the last few years for their lack of transparency when it comes to charges and fees. Anne Kates Smith, senior editor for Kiplinger's Personal Finance magazine, had the following to say about this in an article entitled "Mutual Funds' Hidden Fees" in its September 2011 issue:

> "Depending on how trigger-happy a fund's manager is, trading costs can prove a formidable hurdle for returns to overcome. Trading costs are among the most opaque because they're not reported as part of a fund's expense ratio the same way that other costs of running the fund are. Funds must disclose the brokerage commissions they pay, but most times you have to hunt the disclosure down in a fund's statement of additional information."

One important factor to consider is this: mutual funds are subject to market risk. If the stock market is on a roll and your account is growing, you probably won't mind the fees. When the market is down and your account is losing value, you can't easily find the charges. So, either way, you don't see how much owning the mutual fund is costing you. It would be nice to be able to view one of these statements and see a big heading in bold print: **FEES AND OTHER CHARGES.** But that is unlikely. The fees seem to be intentionally camouflaged so you won't notice them. Here is what you are paying your brokerage firm over and above your mutual fund sales commissions:

Revenue-sharing fee. This is a fee the management company of each mutual fund pays the broker for "marketing." It can range between 0.10 percent and 0.40 percent of your assets, so a 0.20 percent fee is generating $60 a year from a $30,000 account. This is a hidden cost, but you can be sure you're paying it.

Account maintenance fee. A broker charges an average of $20 to "maintain" each mutual fund in your account. This fee is paid annually by a mutual fund to your broker. If you hold four mutual funds, your broker is paid $80 a year.

Shareholder servicing fee. Under current regulatory rules, a mutual fund can pay a broker up to 0.25 percent of your assets for "servicing" your account. If you have a $30,000 account balance, that's $75 a year.

These fees are a few of the most egregious. And if you just add up the fees in this example, your broker is receiving as much as $215 a year to oversee four mutual fund investments. That may not sound like a lot of money, but on average these fees and charges add up to more than 50 basis points of your assets each year. So if you expect to earn, let's say 5 percent per year on your investments, these extra fees mean you are losing out on 10 percent of whatever that 5 percent return equals in asset gains. Remember, these fees are on top of sales commission or other fees you might pay the broker for advice.

The purpose of fine print is not always to save paper. Sure, you can usually find these fees in the disclosure documents, but people usually don't read them and, if they do, they don't generally understand the terms. The fund prospectus may contain a "statement of additional information," but from our experience, it is the last place investors look. In our experience as financial advisers, we have yet to interview anyone who fully understood how much they were paying for their mutual funds. Most of those surveyed said they did not even read the summary prospectus, let alone the full prospectus.

Sometimes information is further concealed in the fine print of a broker's website. Some of the funds brokers recommend to their clients do pretty well, but many others don't and you are still saddled with the expensive cost structure either way.

CHAPTER FIVE

The Truth About Annuities

It seems that every time we research anything having to do with annuities on the internet, we encounter misinformation. Sometimes claims are so biased and blatantly untrue that it's like some mischievous gremlin is purposely planting lies and half-truths to deceive and confuse. Hopefully this chapter will shed some light on the subject and chase at least some of those gremlins away.

The word "annuity" is like the word "automobile." Just as there are many types of automobiles and many manufacturers of automobiles, there are many types of annuities and many companies that design and market them. Driving a one-passenger racecar is quite different from driving a family sedan, but they are both automobiles. And within those extremes, driving a Ford sedan is quite different from driving a Mercedes. Similarly, one annuity can be so completely different in features, benefits and structure from another annuity that it should have a different name. When you see the word annuity, look for one of the following words that describe **what type** of annuity is being discussed. Each is different in many ways.

- Immediate annuity
- Fixed annuity
- Fixed index annuity
- Variable annuity

Regardless of what stripe they are, all annuities do have the following things in common:

- They are issued by insurance companies
- All types of fixed annuities (deferred, immediate, index) offer guarantees* of principal by the issuing insurance company
- Benefits may pass immediately to heirs at death (without probate)
- Earnings are normally tax-deferred, meaning they are taxed as ordinary income when withdrawn, but not before

Wasn't it Shakespeare who made that famous, profound observation that "a rose by any other name would smell as sweet?" Just as an experiment, and to demonstrate how bias, no matter how unfounded, can influence our opinions, we asked a group of people to tell us what their idea of a perfect investment would be. We listed the attributes of this perfect investment on a whiteboard. When we boiled it down, here's the way it looked:

1. Full liquidity – Get your money out any time without paying a penalty for early withdrawal.

2. Complete safety – No way you can lose your principle. Fully guaranteed.

3. High rate of return – Either a double-digit fixed interest rate that cannot be changed, or following the stock market when it goes up but not when it goes down.

4. Tax free – You don't have to share any of your gains with Uncle Sam, either while they are accruing or when you withdraw them.

After we had drawn up the investment on the board we asked the audience what we should call our creation.

"Utopia," said an eager woman on the front row. A man in the back nailed it, however. "Impossible!" he called out.

And he's right, of course. Such an investment does not exist. When it comes to investing, there is usually always a tradeoff. To illustrate: A small, family-run hardware store was losing customers to one of the chain hardware stores in a small town. Especially irksome to the owner was when old customers would visit his store to learn how to perform some do-it-yourself task and then visit the megastore to purchase the hardware to do the job – all because the items there were a bit cheaper. So the owner put up a sign above the cash register that read: *"Quality Hardware, Great Service, Low Prices – Pick Any Two."*

In investing, everything is a tradeoff. Higher interest rates are usually accompanied by a longer term of investment. That's why a five-year CD usually yields more than a one-year CD. Shorter-term investments with great liquidity are usually accompanied by lower rates of return. Higher returns are usually accompanied by higher risk.

To carry the experiment a little further, we asked the audience to tell us what they thought of putting their money in what we would call "Investment X."

Investment X

"Investment X" will provide returns with little or no downside risk. Your returns will be linked to the performance of an index, such as the S&P 500, the Dow Jones Industrial Average or the Nasdaq, or maybe even a combination of indices. Your account will rise in value when the index rises, up to a cap of, let's say 2-4 percent. But when the market falls, your gains are locked in. You can never go backward.

"Investment X" is tax deferred. In other words, you will never owe taxes on your gains as long as you simply hold onto the contract. That means the gains are free to compound, along with the rest of the money invested, as long as they are not withdrawn.

When you do withdraw money from the contract, it will be taxed as ordinary income.

"Investment X" will carry with it three different levels of guarantees to ensure that you never lose your principle due to market volatility. The worst you can do in a year when the market tanks is zero growth. No more sleepless nights during a severe market downturn, worrying about losing your nest egg.

"Investment X" has no additional fees. No maintenance fee, no investment fees, no hidden fees and no trading commissions. What you see is what you get. The only fee you would pay is if you elected to have an optional rider that would guarantee you a lifetime income that you could not outlive. The amount of the income would be based on your age and how long your investment had been in place. The optional rider isn't free; it is usually in the neighborhood of 1 percent of the account value per year.

"Investment X" would be transferrable to your named beneficiaries upon your death. Any portion of the account you didn't use could be left to your loved ones without having to go through probate courts. It would not be tax free, as in life insurance death benefits, but its gains would be taxed as ordinary income upon withdrawal.

Now by a Show of Hands...

"Now, by a show of hands, how many would like an investment like Investment X?" Almost every hand went up.

"By a show of hands, how many here like annuities?"

Eight hands went up, representing about one-fourth of the audience. As it turns out, these were people who had annuities and were pleased with their performance.

When we told the group that Investment X is a *fixed index annuity,* there were surprised looks and at least one audible gasp.

We will describe in detail exactly what a fixed index annuity is and how it works, but we thought it was an interesting experiment to present it in a plain brown wrapper first. It reveals something about preconceived notions. Sometimes, we become so conditioned by opinions expressed in the media or by the opinions of other individuals that we can end up with a mind that is made up and doesn't want to be confused with the facts. For years, many in the mainstream financial world of brokers and Wall Streeters have been casting insurance products such as annuities and life insurance in a bad light, not because these concepts and products are not effective, but because they don't market them. It's like asking a Chevy dealer to rate Ford products, or vice versa.

So, follow the money trail; most of the advice put forth by the talking heads on television and in the columns of financial journals is influenced by the profit motives of advertisers. Professional people who have been educated in one school of thought are not likely to sing the praises of another. That's true in just about every field – medical, financial, musical, even agricultural.

For example, a friend of ours suffered from lower back pain. He went to a lumbar specialist who diagnosed it as a slipped disc. This doctor had performed many spinal surgeries and told our friend that he could expect to have a back operation within a couple of years to correct the problem. In the meantime, she prescribed a back brace and pain medication. Our friend next visited a homeopathic chiropractor who told him that regular visits and an hour each week on the adjustment table coupled with stretching exercises was the key to recovery. Both doctors advised him to lose weight. Our friend lost 30 pounds, took the pain medication, did the stretches, had the adjustments and wore the back brace. Guess what? The pain went away and hasn't recurred. What does that prove? Simply that, when there are two diametrically opposed schools of thought on a common problem, the truth is sometimes in the middle. Which doctor was right? Both of them. But don't expect them to attend the same medical conferences or ever to work in the same office.

Annuities are not suitable for every client, but brokers tend to have tunnel vision when discussing them. Market-based investments carry risk, but they can offer tremendous growth potential, especially once the lifetime income piece of the retirement puzzle is in place. When two otherwise reasonable professionals attack the programs of each other like two elks battling on the tundra during mating season, one has to draw the conclusion that profit motive figures in there somewhere. As psychologist and philosopher Abram Maslow said, "If you only have a hammer, you tend to see every problem as a nail."

Much of what is written on financial topics is written by journalists who do not have degrees in finance or economics. They usually develop their material by interviewing "experts" on the phone. Through no fault of their own, they are usually not allowed the time to really understand the layers of complexity that surround the topics on which they write. It has been our observation that they often tell half the story when it comes to annuities, or confuse one type of annuity with another. Sometimes their opinions are outdated. And some just get it all wrong. The only problem is that people tend to take what's in print for gospel.

Sifting Through the Noise

Right after the economic meltdown of 2008, when many saw how vulnerable their life's savings could be when exposed to the vagaries of a volatile stock market, millions of American investors went running to the safety and guaranteed growth of annuities. Naturally, that didn't sit too well with advisers from the traditional, market-based investing world. The financial magazines were splashed with articles vilifying annuities. But the proof of the pudding was in the eating. Those who sought the safety of insurance-based retirement products benefitted from the move. Their thriving portfolios began to capture the attention of unbiased financial writers and many of them retracted earlier articles demonizing annuities – a trend which we see continuing. But let us go on record to say that we do not endorse any one approach or any one product. We believe in what works for our clients and ultimately what honors their wishes once they understand all viable options.

The History of Annuities

Annuities trace their origins back to ancient Rome when they were known as *annua*, which is Latin for "annual stipends." Roman citizens would make a one-time payment to the *annua*, in exchange for lifetime payments made once a year. During the "dark ages" the idea died out and did not surface again until the 17th century when annuities were used as fund-raising vehicles to pay for wars. European governments created the "*tontine*," a form of annuity, which promised an extended annual payout in the future in return for contributions made now.

Annuities surfaced in America in 1759 when Presbyterian ministers were allowed to participate in an annuity to benefit their families. In 1812 the Pennsylvania Company for Insurances on Lives and Granting Annuities was the first commercial annuity offered to the general public.[6] From that point on, annuity growth was steady, but really caught on in the days of the Great Depression, when banks and other investment vehicles had failed.[7] The New Deal Program introduced by President Franklin D. Roosevelt during that era contained programs that encouraged individuals to save for their own retirement.

Today's annuities bear a resemblance to the annuities of yesteryear, but it is like comparing the horsepower of a modern V-8 engine to that of a Model T. Traditional annuities remained essentially unchanged throughout the 19th and most of the 20th

---

[6] Michael Lustig. Cal-State Exams, Real Estate License Services, Inc. 2009. "Annuity Training." https://books.google.com/books?id=ND9qqhk56R4C. Accessed Dec. 9, 2016.

centuries. The old annuities were bare-bones affairs. Similar to today's traditional fixed annuities, they offered a guaranteed return of principal, a fixed rate of return, a payout choice of (a) life or (b) a certain number of years. There were few bells and whistles to choose from. If you chose the payout, you forfeited control of the account. If you lived a long time after opting for the lifetime payout, for example, you won. If you died early, the insurance company kept the balance in the account.

The thing about annuities that continued to attract investors was their tax-deferred status. This feature allowed annuity owners to put the time value of money to work for them with greater force. Then in 1952 the first variable annuity was created.[8]

Variable Annuities

Variable annuities are essentially market investments with tax-deferred growth and some guarantees that only insurance companies could provide, such as death benefits. All goes well in a booming economy when the direction of the market remains upward. But variable annuities can lose value during a downturn. You could say that variable annuities combine an investment account with the equivalent of an insurance policy. On the upside, they appeal to middle-aged investors with a promise of a guaranteed retirement paycheck that could reset higher if the underlying investments fare well. On the downside, they usually come with higher fees than fixed annuities.

While compiling information for this book, we came across some articles that indicate changes are taking place with variable annuities that are causing concern for some who own them. Kelly Green and Leslie Scism wrote an article entitled "They're Changing Our Annuity," which appeared in the Wall Street Journal in

---

[8] Ibid.

April 2013. They pointed out that low long-term interest rates are "bringing out the stingy side of some insurers."

"Those companies that offered unusually generous guarantees on their (variable) annuities are now worried about their own financial health," the article stated. "As a result, some insurers are changing annuity contracts. The moves include clamping down on fund choices, raising fees, blocking additional account contributions and, in some cases, trying to buy back the contracts."[9]

Forbes magazine ran a headline on July 2, 2012, that read: "9 Reasons You Need to Avoid Variable Annuities." The article went on to proclaim: "Suze Orman doesn't like them. Some journalists are suspicious of them. Fee-only financial advisers generally avoid them."[10]

Why the negative sentiment? The main reason is that your money is at risk. This showed up loud and clear during the last market crash when these accounts lost billions in their base accounts. They have also been chastised for being very expensive and containing confusing income riders that produce "pension Income" as a means of "guaranteeing growth."

We are the front lines of all things financial, so we hear the complaints firsthand. Some will ask us, "What is going on with my variable annuity? I'm not making any money. In fact, I've lost money!"

Many aren't aware of what their internal rate of return is. They also are quite alarmed to find out how expensive their variable annuity is. Here is an example: The average annual fee is 3.5 percent. Let say you have $500,000 invested in a VA. $500,000 x

---

[9] Kelly Green, Leslie Scism. Wall Street Journal. April 19, 2013. "They're Changing Our Annuity!" http://www.wsj.com/articles/SB100014241278873243458045784269405 60031964. Accessed Dec. 9, 2016.

[10] Eve Kaplan. Forbes. July 2, 2012. "9 Reasons You Need to Avoid Variable Annuities." http://www.forbes.com/sites/feeonlyplanner/2012/07/02/9-reasons-you-need-to-avoid-variable-annuities/#3fe491524d62. Accessed Dec. 9, 2016.

0.035= $17,500 in fees. Over 10 years, that is $175,000. Add $50,000 in growth over that time and the balance is $375,000!

One spinoff from the variable annuity that has been adopted and modified by the fixed annuity crowd is the guaranteed lifetime income rider. This relatively new development seems to scratch baby boomers just where they itch when it comes creating their own pension. When "income riders" were added to fixed index annuities in the mid-2000s, it was like the union of chocolate and peanut butter for baby boomers, most of whom had been looking for ways to keep their nest egg safe and create their own pension.

Fixed Index Annuities

Remember back in the 1990s when you could do no wrong in the stock market? You could pick just about any stock (especially tech stocks) and you were almost guaranteed a profit. With so much money to be made in the stock market, it is no wonder that baby boomers, who were at the peak of their investing years, found the old-style traditional fixed annuities with their fixed interest rates boring and unattractive.

Sure, the idea of a lifetime income stream may have been appealing, but under the terms of the traditional fixed annuity, if you wanted to convert the annuity to an income stream you had to *annuitize* the contract. That is, give up control of your principal forever. Let's say, for instance, that a 65-year-old converted a $300,000 traditional fixed annuity to a lifetime income stream of, say, $20,000 per year. If he or she were to die in a car accident a month later, according to the conditions of the contract, the income stream would stop. Would the annuitant's beneficiaries get the balance? Nope. Nary a penny. This presented a problem for baby boomers who had come of age in the Wall Street boom years. As the 20th century came to an end, and the younger generation of investors began thinking seriously about retirement, they seemed to want the best of both worlds. On the one hand, they liked the safety of fixed annuities and the idea of a lifetime income stream. On the other hand, they liked the upside potential of the stock market. So, insurance companies, who, just like the banks and Wall Street, were in competition for the boomers' retirement savings dollars, ordered their product-design people and actuaries to retool the traditional fixed annuity. What came out of those re-design sessions was something unique – the *fixed index annuity*. The most innovative feature of the FIA? The ratchet-reset method of producing gains. Instead of using the fixed rates of the traditional fixed annuity, the FIA would track a stock market index such as the S&P 500, tabulate the growth at the end of the annuity's contract year, and credit gains to the annuity accordingly. When the market went up, your annuity balance would likewise rise. But when the market receded, you would not participate in those losses. Your gains would lock in while you waited for the next upswing – thus the term "ratchet/reset." It worked on the same principle as a ratchet mechanism on a machine. Force exerted in one direction is not exerted in the other.

Sound too good to be true? It is if we left it there. Uncapped gains would bankrupt the insurance companies in short order, so the product-design people put an adjustable ceiling on the gains. For example, if the market rose 25 percent one year, your gains would be capped at, say, 6 percent. The insurance company could adjust the cap each year depending on the prevailing interest rate and the overall economy.

The "REAL BENEFITS"
of Indexed Annuities with the Annual Reset Design

A history of American Equity's Index-5® (9/30/98 - 9/30/15)

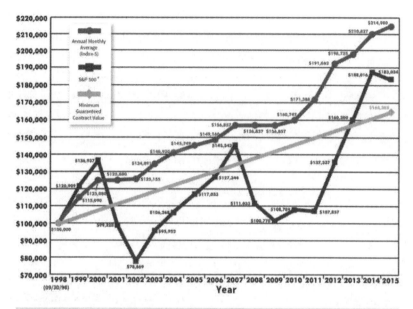

Source: American Equity

Why Call It a "Fixed Index Annuity?"

Fixed: Like its predecessor, the traditional fixed annuity, the principal is fixed. Unlike its distant cousin, the variable annuity, the principal cannot be eroded by changes in the stock market or dips in the economy.

Index: Returns can be linked to the upward movement of a stock market index, such as the S&P 500, the Dow or a combination of several indices. FIA owners are not "invested" directly in the stock market. Insurance companies merely use these indexes, or barometers of market activity, to as the measuring stick by which to attribute gains to the account each year.

Annuity: It is an annuity. The main purpose of any annuity is to provide income. Like other annuities, growth within the FIA is tax deferred. Like other annuities, the FIA is capable of providing an income stream to its owner. Like all other annuities, FIAs have surrender periods. Most contracts allow for the contract holder to withdraw up to 10 percent of the account balance per year: more than that and you may incur extra charges until your surrender period expires. FIA surrender charges and surrender periods vary from carrier to carrier. A typical surrender period is 10 years; some longer, some shorter. The penalty for early withdrawal is usually presented in descending percentages as the surrender period expires.

How have FIAs been received by Americans? According to LIMRA, an independent research organization, FIA sales reached $48.2 billion in 2014. That was $9 billion higher than previous year and a 23 percent increase from 2013. In 2014, FIAs held more than 50 percent market share of all fixed annuity sales.

What about variable annuities? LIMRA reported the following: "Variable annuity (VA) sales fell 4 percent in 2014, totaling $140.1 billion. This represents the lowest annual VA sales since 2009. VA sales were $34.2 billion in the fourth quarter, down 6 percent from the prior year."[11]

Looking Under the Hood

When the insurance industry boosted the horsepower of the annuity in the 1990s, they also made it more complex, just like modern-day automobile engines. But, just like some car buyers like to understand what makes the engine tick, some annuity buyers may wish to check "under the hood" of these financial products

---

[11] LIMRA. Feb. 23, 2015. "Total U.S. Annuity Sales Improve Three Percent in 2014." http://www.limra.com/Posts/PR/News_Releases/Total_U_S_Annuity_Sales _Improve_Three_Percent_in_2014.aspx. Accessed Aug. 24, 2016.

and see the inner workings. If you are *not* the engineer type, you may wish to skip to the next chapter. But for the others, we will outline some of the inner workings of the FIA.

Crediting Strategies

With traditional fixed annuities, what you saw (the declared interest rate) was what you got. But since FIAs track the upward movement of a stock index, the annuitant has the option of fine tuning the crediting strategies each year, usually when the contract's anniversary date rolls around. The simplest strategy is **annual point-to-point.** That means you look at the index at the beginning of the contract year, look at it again when the year ends, and calculate the percentage of change. If the ending index value is up, your gains are calculated on the difference. If the index is down, you don't lose. Zero is your hero in a down market year.

Conservative investors may wish to use the **fixed strategy.** Suppose you just had a gut feeling that the market was heading for a down year. You could opt for the fixed strategy. The annuity would behave similar to traditional fixed annuities and return a fixed rate of, say, 3 percent or so. Not sure? Want to "hedge your bets?" You could split it 50-50, or 75-25, or any other combination, between the annual point-to-point and the fixed strategy.

The reason for so many options is to give FIA owners as much control over the contract as possible. Some choose to "set it on autopilot" and forget it. Enjoy the beach, or their golf game, and let their adviser worry about the fine tuning. We completely understand that. But others who are market savvy and love details may wish to tinker with them, which is also perfectly understandable

Other Strategies

Some annuity carriers offer a **monthly average** wherein the insurance company tracks the values of the index on a monthly basis for a year. At the end of the year, they add them up and divide by 12. They subtract the starting value from the monthly average. That figure is divided by the value of the index at the start of the year to calculate the yearly returns. Complicated? Perhaps, but some like this method and think it works well in a volatile market.

The ***monthly sum strategy*** calls for comparing the index value of each month with the one just prior. Add up the increases and decreases at the end of the year and if the result is positive, then that is the amount credited to your account. If it is negative, then zero is your hero. At least you didn't lose. This strategy is favored by those who feel the market will continue in a steady upward trend.

We realize your head may be spinning from information overload at this point, but just like you don't have be able to name and identify all the parts of a car engine to enjoy its performance, you don't have to be able to take a fixed index annuity apart and put it back together again to own one. But if we are about anything, it is full disclosure and complete transparency. The reason why insurance companies designed so many options is not to confuse you, but to help you and your adviser achieve your specific financial goals. It is a way to get as much as possible from the stock market without taking undue risk.

Hybrid Annuities

You may hear the term "hybrid annuities" when these products are discussed. A hybrid is two things combined. When people use it in reference to an annuity, they are usually referring to a **fixed index annuity** combined with an **income rider.** A good illustration is a sidecar (income rider) attached to a motorcycle (annuity). You cannot operate a sidecar independent of the motorcycle, but you can operate the motorcycle without a sidecar. For the income rider to work, you must have the base annuity to go with it. Most

(69 percent according to LIMRA) fixed index annuities come with income riders these days.[12]

Like hybrid cars, hybrid annuities have two engines:

- **Base account value**
- **Income account value**

They each function differently, but together they provide the "horsepower" for the hybrid annuity. Here's an example:

Let's say you deposit $500,000 and the insurance company adds a 10 percent bonus. Right off the bat, both accounts total $550,000. The *base account value* grows based on the stock market index. The *income account value* is essentially a "ledger account," and is not accessible as a lump sum. It usually grows at a fixed rate (declared in the contract). The industry term for this rate is the "roll-up" rate. More details on that later.

The only purpose of the income account is – you guessed it – to provide income. The income rider is a far cry from annuitization, where you sacrificed control of the balance of the annuity in return for a lifetime income. With these annuities, if you were to die a month after starting your lifetime income payments, your beneficiaries would receive whatever was left of the base account value according to the terms of the contract. Some income riders come with optional provisions that pay for long-term care in either lump sums or payments.

It seems there are as many variations and permutations to the income riders as there are to the annuities themselves. They are called by several names, too:

- **GLIR** – Guaranteed Lifetime Income Rider
- **GLIB** – Guaranteed Lifetime Income Benefit
- **GLWB** – Guaranteed Lifetime Withdrawal Benefit

---

[12] LIMRA. Nov. 18, 2014. "LIMRA Secure Retirement Institute: Total Annuity Sales Fall Two Percent in Third Quarter." http://www.limra.com/Posts/PR/News_Releases/LIMRA_Secure_Retirement_Institute___Total_Annuity_Sales_Fall_Two_Percent_in_Third_Quarter.aspx. Accessed Aug. 24, 2016.

Are income riders free? No, but they aren't terribly expensive, either. Typically, they are 1 percent or thereabouts of the annuity balance, annually. Sometimes this cost is expressed outright, or it can be shown as reduced returns. For example, if the annuity earns 6 percent interest one year, and the constant cost of the income rider is 90 bps (basis points), then the net return of the annuity that year would be 5.10 percent.

The *'roll-up rate"* mentioned earlier is another term you hear when these products are discussed. The income account value begins with the same value as the base account and then "rolls up" (accrues interest) at a rate set by the insurance company. This rate will vary from one contract to another and can be anywhere from 5-7 percent, depending on how your annuity is structured. Typically, once these rates are locked in place, they remain fixed until the income is triggered, or until the end of the roll-up period (usually 10 years). After the roll-up period expires, the annuity owner can extend it for another period at whatever rate is declared at that time.

The "G" in the GLIB, GLIR, GLWB

Most of the acronyms used for income riders start with the letter "G," which stands for guaranteed. How does that work? Annuities aren't backed by the Federal Deposit Insurance Corporation like bank CDs. So how can they claim the income riders are "guaranteed?" The insurance company itself provides several layers of guarantees:

- **Reserves.** The claims-paying capability of the insurance company itself is measured in the amount of reserves it maintains. This is regulated by the states in which the insurance company operates. Unlike banks, insurance companies are required by law to keep a portion of their assets unencumbered to protect policy holders and keep themselves from default. These backup funds can be in cash or marketable securities.

- **Reinsurance.** Insurance companies buy insurance from other insurance companies to provide backup for their contracts.
- **Legal Reserve System.** State departments of insurance require insurance companies to participate in the legal reserve pool before they are allowed to do business in that state. Insurance company failures are rare, but it can happen. With the Legal Reserve System, if an insurance company fails, other insurance companies may buy the failed insurance company's book of business and carry out the defunct insurance companies promises.

Distribution Formulas

To understand how FIAs with income riders work, think of a massive dam. You created the dam when you purchased the annuity. Behind the dam is a large lake, formed by your initial deposit and the interest accrued. This is your base account value. In front of the dam is a dry river bed, which represents your eventual income stream. Naturally, the longer you allow the dam to collect water, the larger your lake. But the size of your riverbed is based on a fixed calculation of your income account value and your age in a formula provided in your contract. So, if you have allowed your income account value to accumulate at its fixed rate for longer, then your riverbed will be bigger. When you turn the income on, it will initially flow out of your lake, decreasing your base account value. Yet, the riverbed will maintain its steady flow.

What happens if you start your income stream and die prematurely? Who gets the money represented by the lake in the above illustration? Your beneficiaries do. Then again, what happens if you live to be 100, and the income stream has long since drained the lake dry? Congratulations are in order. You lived a long life. The insurance company's obligation to you in this case was to continue filling the riverbed, even after your lake went dry (and it probably cost them dearly). There is no more money left for your beneficiaries. You used it all!

We mentioned income formulas associated with income riders. They can vary from company to company, but the typical formula goes like this: if you are between the ages of 60 and 70 years of age your income will likely be 5 percent of your "ledger" account value *at the point where you opted to turn on the income.* You choose your payment frequency: Do you want annual income? Monthly? Quarterly? What if you start your income between the ages of 70 and 80? A typical formula would allow you to receive 6 percent of your income base account, *at the point where you opted to turn on the income,* for life.

One more point of interest for you engineer types. If your base account value is higher than your income account value, most contracts allow you to use the higher of the two accounts as a calculation base. Once you trigger the income, that amount is locked in for life. Some companies have optional inflation provisions.

Please remember, even as detailed as the description offered here is, it is still just an overview. It is impossible to do more than cover the basics here. But any competent adviser should be able to answer all your specific questions.

CHAPTER SIX

Saying Goodbye to the 4% Rule

What does the 4 percent rule have in common with dial-up modems and flip phones? They are all things that worked well in the 1990s but are laughably out of date today. It used to be that the "holy grail" of retirement analysis was something called "the 4 percent sustainable withdrawal rule." The theory was, if you withdraw an income of 4 percent per year from your retirement account and rebalance the portfolio as you get older, you will be able to live comfortably throughout an average retirement without running out of money. The 4 percent rule was put forth in the 1990s by stock brokers and is still preached as gospel by some in the financial advisory community. But the math just doesn't work with the new economy of the 21st century, and most of the faithful have left the faith.

The 4 percent concept was developed in1994 by three professors at San Antonio's Trinity University whose aim was to figure out how much money one could take out of a stock market account each year in retirement, all the while adjusting the balance between stocks and bonds, and not run out of money. They tinkered with the math and, based on projections rooted in historical performance, they declared that the magic number was 4-5 percent on the outside. But this came with a lot of assumptions. First of all, the market had to perform according to their projections, which were based on a 70-year look-back. Since they took those measurements in 1995, it's no wonder that the 4 percent theory worked. In the 1990s, the stock market was a thoroughbred stallion with blinders on. It only knew one direction – up! Any market investment you made in those heady days fared well. When you looked at the market long term, the only hiccup since the Great Depression of the 1930s occurred in 1987, and even then it recovered quickly. These three professors had no way of knowing that two severe market crashes would occur in the next 15 years, resulting in the "lost decade" of the 2000s when the market neither gained nor lost, despite unsettling volatility.

The work of the three professors attracted a lot of attention by the Wall Street crowd and became known as the "Trinity Study." There was nothing essentially wrong with the research they did in search of what they called a "sustainable withdrawal rate." The market sample they used went as far back as possible, all the way from 1925 up to 1995. They also used five different portfolio compositions – 100 percent stocks, 100 percent bonds, and 25/75, 50/50 and 75/25 mixes. They tinkered with the numbers to see which withdrawal rates would leave these portfolios with positive values at the end of 15, 20, 25 and 30 years, and 4 percent turned out to be the magic number based on the data they had at hand.

In 1994, a CPA by the name of Bill Bengen published a landmark article in the Journal of Financial Planning and presented his own findings in the search for the sustainable withdrawal rate. Bengen's approach was to use the same market history but to factor in the "what ifs" of extended bear markets, minimal stock market gains and sustained high inflation. Even with those variables added in, Bengen concluded that a retiree who was 50-75 percent invested in stocks should draw down a portfolio by no more than 4 percent per year to make their retirement money last a lifetime.

People began to call Bengen's theory the "4 percent drawdown rule" and it was soon adopted as an industry standard.

What Went Wrong?

So what happened? Why were these sharp minds so far off the mark when people in the 21st century actually started retiring and counting on the 4 percent rule to carry them through?

The market crashes of 2000 and 2008 happened. What no one had figured on was a prolonged market rout in the first two or three years of retirement and how that would skew the numbers.

Stock Market Performance Over Last 30 Years

Source: Security Benefit

In other words, timing is everything if your retirement nest egg is 100 percent invested in stocks, bonds and mutual funds. Let's face it. If you lose 40 percent of your nest egg right after you retire, which many people did, the 4 percent rule goes right out the window. If you had retired Jan. 1, 2000, for example, with a portfolio of 55 percent stocks and 45 percent bonds and re-balanced the portfolio each month and increased the withdrawal amount by 3 percent each year for inflation, which is what the 4 percent rule calls for, your portfolio would still have fallen by a third through 2010, according to investment firm T. Rowe Price Group. They estimated that your chances of making it through three decades of retirement would be only 29 percent.

We don't know about you, but if we were to go up to the ticket counter at an airport and the ticket agent told us that the plane had a 29 percent chance of landing at its destination, we wouldn't fly on that plane.

So that's the problem; what's the solution?

Reporter Kelley Greene, who has covered the retirement scene since 2000 for the Wall Street Journal, in an article that appeared March 1, 2013, suggests one alternative could be using annuities with income riders. She quotes Wade Pfau, a professor who researches retirement income at the American College of Financial Services in Bryn Mawr, Pennsylvania, and who holds a Ph.D. in economics from Princeton University. The professor plotted how 1,001 different product allocations might work for a 65-year-old married couple hoping to generate 4 percent annual income from their portfolio. Using 200 Monte Carlo simulations for each product, and assuming returns based on current market conditions, the winning combination turned out to be a 50/50 mix of stocks and fixed annuities. "Annuities, with their promise of income for life, act like 'super bonds with no maturity dates,' [Pfau] says."[13]

Sequence of Returns

As some of the brightest minds in economics figured out, when it comes to using at-risk funds in retirement, timing can be critical. An expression making the rounds these days is "sequence of

---

[13] Kelley Greene. Wall Street Journal. March 1, 2013. "Say Goodbye to the 4% Rule." http://www.wsj.com/articles/SB10001424127887324162304578304491492559684. Accessed Aug. 24, 2016.

returns." This is from a GAO retirement income report released in 2013. It said, in summary, if you have some early losses in your portfolio, such as 2001, 2002 or 2008, then it will affect the longevity of that portfolio if you continue drawing the same amount from the account each year, as in the 4 percent scenario discussed earlier. In other words, if you have early losses, your money may only last 18 years instead of 20. But if you have those same losses later on in retirement, that same portfolio may last 24 years. It all about the *sequence* in which you experienced those losses.

As the term implies, sequence risk, or sequence of returns risk, has to do with the order in which your investment returns occur. When you are in the accumulation or savings stage, sequence risk does not affect you. It is something you experience when you transition from contributing to your retirement nest egg into needing to draw income from your investments.

The best way to see this in action is to imagine that we have two investors. We will call them Jim and Andy. They both reach age 65 with identical nest eggs of $500,000 each, solely invested in the stock market. Now they start taking annual withdrawals of 5 percent from their accounts. Let's kick in a 3 percent increase each year for inflation. While this is happening, they each average an 8.03 percent annual return. Each of them experienced three consecutive years of significant market losses (If that scenario sounds familiar, that's what happened in years 2000-2003.)

Please understand – and this is important – these two investors are not mirrors of each other. We didn't say that the three consecutive years happened at the ***same time!***

Jim's stock market losses:

-10.14% at age 65

-13.04% at age 66

-23.37% at age 67

Andy's stock market losses:

-23.37% at age 87

-13.04% at age 88

-10.14% at age 89

How Jim and Andy were affected by the sequence of returns

By age 68, after three straight years of market losses, plus the withdrawals, Jim's $500,000 account had shrunk to around $250,000. Andy's account, however, was up over $750,000 when he was 68. By the time he was 86, his account was up to over $2 million. Then three years of losses took it down to around $1.5 million at age 89. Jim's account never quite recovered from the losses experienced so early in retirement. He ran out of money at age 83.

They were different ages when those losses occurred. Because the three-year period of losses occurred near the beginning for Jim, his account suffered badly, whereas Andy, who experienced the same losses, but toward the end of the retirement period, was virtually unscathed. Jim had more to lose than Andy just because of the sequence of returns. Jim took the hit in his account between the ages of 65 and 67. Andy's account lost money three years in a row when he was between the ages of 87 and 89. You don't have to be a rocket scientist or a math whiz to see who ran out of money first.

That's why we call it the "sequence of returns *trap.*" Bad timing can wipe out years of careful investing and diligent saving and increase the risk that you will run either run out of money prematurely or wipe out the legacy you had wished to leave to your loved ones.

Knowing how much you need to retire still boils down

to projecting your future expenses until the day you die. In a perfect world, you would amass $1 million, the stock market would dependably go up 8 percent per year, and you would draw 4 percent per year from your nest egg and leave the remainder there to grow. That would give you an annual stipend of $40,000 plus your Social Security and any other sources of income you may have. But a perfect world doesn't exist. So, the way to ensure a comfortable lifestyle that can last you throughout retirement comes down to sensible planning, saving and making prudent investment choices.

Dollar-Cost Averaging

Another example of how timing is everything when it comes to investing is dollar-cost averaging. Dollar-cost averaging is a technique designed to reduce market risk through the systematic purchase of securities at predetermined intervals and set amounts. Many successful investors already practice dollar-cost averaging without realizing it. Let's say you have a job at ABC Corporation and each time you get your paycheck, a portion of it comes out and goes into your 401(k). The custodian who handles your retirement account typically uses that contribution to purchase shares of a mutual fund. When the market is in a downturn, the contribution buys more shares because shares are cheaper. When the market is on an upswing, the contribution buys fewer shares because the shares are more expensive. Those cheaper shares will increase in value when the market recovers. When the market goes up, your account rises with that tide, so you can't complain about that. The investor who is consistently investing the same amount month after month, year after year, is protected from a volatile market. This is one reason we say that time is on the side of the younger stock market investors if they are patient and consistent. Instead of investing assets in a lump sum, the investor works his way into a position by slowly buying smaller amounts over a longer period, spreading out the cost basis over several years.

Reverse Dollar-Cost Averaging

It's ironic in a way, but the insulation of dollar-cost averaging that protects younger investors during their working years can come back to haunt them when they move from the accumulation stage of life to the preservation and distribution phase. You could be the victim of **reverse** dollar-cost averaging. Let's say that you are in full retirement. When you stopped working for ABC Corporation, you stopped contributing to the company-sponsored 401(k) retirement savings program as well. Now the money river begins flowing the other way. You must now begin withdrawing from the fund you used to contribute to. You are essentially replacing the paycheck you used to receive with your own, nonrenewable resources. Those withdrawals are made with the same regularity as your earlier deposits were made, only now the withdrawals are much more. You are no longer buying shares; you are selling them each time you withdraw. When the price of those shares fluctuate, which they will always do, you still write yourself the same paycheck each month from your retirement account. So, if the share prices go up, you sell fewer shares. If the share prices go down, you sell more shares. If the market crashes, the value of your account goes down dramatically. Those losses are more hurtful because time is no longer on your side. You are no longer buying cheaper shares that will eventually gain back their value. When share prices drop, you must sell more of those cheap shares to draw the same amount from the account. You must also factor in that you are depleting the account at a faster rate and that every share you sell is one less share that will be working for you in the account.

CHAPTER SEVEN

Weathering the Perfect Storm

'Government s view of the economy could be summed up in a few short phrases: If it moves, tax it. If it keeps moving, regulate it. And if it stops moving, subsidize it."~Ronald Reagan

The Perfect Storm of Nov. 1, 1991, made meteorological history and was the backdrop for a Hollywood motion picture thriller whose main characters were the sea and the hapless and doomed crew of a fishing boat out of Gloucester, Massachusetts.

In October, most of the United States begins to cool down from the summer heat. It can be a tricky weather month for coastal cities because ocean water holds heat longer than the land. This creates massive storms in the Atlantic as winter replaces summer in the still-warm waters. When cold air from Canada moves eastward across the land and meets the warmer ocean air off the New England coast, they form large storms known as Nor'easters. The Perfect Storm was so named because it was the result of a rare convergence of a high-pressure system coming from the south, a low-pressure system coming from Canada, and the remnants from Hurricane Grace moving up from the south. It was a trinity of terror for the fishing vessel Andrea Gail and her crew of nine who disappeared in waves reported to be as much as 100 feet high.

Weather forecasters began warning of this immense storm when New Englanders were enjoying clear bright blue October weather. Damage from the Perfect Storm totaled over $200 million and killed 13 people.

The Perfect Economic Storm

The academics at the University of Pennsylvania's Wharton School of Business watch the economy the same way those New England meteorologists watched the weather in the fall of 1991. They see some scary events taking place – events that seem at first glance to be vaguely related, but when viewed interactively point to a perfect storm of a different kind for retiring Americans – an economic perfect storm. The research of Professors David F. Babbel and Craig B. Merrill identifies several trends that are combining to make retirement in the 21st century more difficult than ever. Here is a summary of some of what they point in their "Investing Your Lump Sum" policy brief:[14]

- Declining returns on Social Security contributions. Compared to earlier generations, today's workers may receive a much lower return on their Social Security contributions. And government projections give reason to doubt the system will be able to continue its current payout rate.

- The decline of traditional pension plans. The number of employer plans that provide retirees with guaranteed retirement income has plummeted from 175,000 in 1983 to fewer than 25,000 today. Many have been replaced by alternatives that help employees to save for retirement, but without the promise of a guaranteed amount of retirement income.

- Increasing life expectancies. For married couples who are both healthy at age 65, there's a 50 percent chance one will live be-

---

[14] David F. Babbel, Craig B. Merrill. Wharton Financial Institutions Center. Aug. 14, 2007. Policy Brief: Personal Finance. "Investing Your Lump Sum at Retirement."

yond 92 and a 25 percent chance that one will live beyond 97. This means your retirement savings may need to last more than 30 years – nearly as long as some Americans' careers.

Reflecting on these trends, Professor Babbel of the Wharton School concludes that outliving one's assets is becoming "the major financial risk of the 21st century." In a 2010 report entitled "Real World Index Annuity Returns," he and his associates identify guaranteed income annuities as a solution, which convert part of your retirement savings into income that will last a lifetime.[15] What's interesting about the Wharton report is that the research is done by professors from one of the most prestigious business schools in the country. They have no merchandise to push, no advertisers to please, and no agenda to promote. In other words, their research into all things pertaining to investment and retirement planning is unbiased and can be obtained by anyone, free of charge.

How much of your retirement savings should be converted into income? As a starting point, the Wharton researchers recommend converting enough of your assets to cover 100 percent of your basic living expenses. Most people already have at least one source of guaranteed income, such as Social Security, employer pensions or military retired pay. These professors maintain that annuities can fill the gap between what these sources of income provide and what you need to retire in comfort and safety.

The GAO Recommendation

Support for using annuities to meet the financial challenges of retirement comes from another source, the Government Accountability Office (GAO). To put it succinctly, the GAO recommends delaying taking Social Security and buying an annuity. Here are

---

[15] David f. Babbel, Jack Marrion, Geoffrey VanderPal. Wharton School. March 4, 2010. "Real World Index Annuity Returns, Revised Version."

some excerpts from the April 2010 report entitled, "Retirement Income: Challenges for Ensuring Income throughout Retirement:"[16]

"Retirees have three primary options to generate a lifetime income stream. First, participants in [defined-benefit] plans can receive their benefits as a lifetime annuity. Second, retirees with [defined-contribution] plan assets can purchase individual life annuities provided by insurance companies that offer retirement income on a lifetime basis. A third option, which would enhance the Social Security lifetime income stream, is to defer retirement under Social Security by a few years (up to age 70) in order to receive higher monthly benefits."

"The risk that retirees will outlive their assets is a growing challenge," said the GAO report, adding that almost half of those nearing retirement will run out of money and will not be able to cover basic expenses and uninsured health-care costs. They concluded that annuities can protect retirees from the risk of outliving their savings.

In one example provided by the GAO, a contract purchased for $95,500 by a 66-year-old couple in Florida may provide $4,262 a year until the death of the surviving spouse and include increases for inflation. The report also recommended that retirees wait until at least full retirement age, or age 66 for those born from 1943 to 1954, before collecting their Social Security benefits. While the Social Security program allows recipients to take reduced payments as early as age 62, it provides full benefits at age 66 and increases payouts by at least 32 percent for those who wait up to age 70.

---

[16] Government Accountability Office. April 28, 2010. "Retirement Income: Challenges for Ensuring Income Throughout Retirement, GAO-10-632R." http://www.gao.gov/assets/100/96692.pdf.

CHAPTER EIGHT

Decisions About Social Security

"Cessation of work is not accompanied by cessation of expenses."
~Cato

On May 10, 1996, a freak spring storm hit Mount Everest, the world's highest mountain, killing five climbers. It had been the deadliest day ever on the famous peak until April 18, 2014, when 16 local guides, called Sherpas, were killed in an avalanche. According to some reports, more than 4,000 people have managed to reach the peak of Mount Everest, and nearly 250 climbers have lost their lives in the attempt.

Climbing Mount Everest is no walk in the park. The peak of Mount Everest is 29,035 feet high and there are several possible routes to it. Deciding which one to take is just one of hundreds of critical decisions climbers must make. Ironically, the route on which the Sherpas were killed in 2014 is considered to be one of the easiest ones to scale. It was the one same one used by Sir Edmund Hillary, the first climber to reach the peak, and his Sherpa, Tenzing Norgay, in 1953.

Scaling Retirement Mountain and getting down the other side safely requires careful decision-making. Take Social Security for example. When should you take it? Some say Social Security may not be around long, so you'd better get it while the getting is good.

"Do the math," said one man who had just turned 62 and was signing up. "Ten thousand people are retiring every day, taking from the system, and fewer people are replacing them to pay into it. How long can that go on?"

We can see why some may wring their hands. But it would be a mistake for baby boomers (those born between 1946 and 1964) to conclude that Social Security will not be there for them. Without a doubt, the system is going to need some adjustments (some of which are being made as we write this) if it is to be here for the children and grandchildren of boomers.

You say you have concerns about the future of Social Security? Apparently the government does too. Here is a paragraph that appears on the front page of 2015 Social Security statements:[17]

> **"About Social Security's Future** - Social Security is a compact between generations. Since 1935, America has kept the promise of security for its workers and their families. Now, however, the Social Security system is facing serious financial problems, and action is needed soon to make sure the system will be sound when today's younger workers are ready for retirement. Without changes, in 2033 the Social Security Trust Fund will be able to pay only about 77 cents for each dollar of scheduled benefits.* We need to resolve these issues soon to make sure Social Security continues to provide a foundation of protection for future generations."

---

[17] Ibid.

Everyone who has contributed into the Social Security system can obtain a copy of his or her Social Security statement. Printed on this three- or four-page report is the amount you stand to receive in the way of benefits. This amount will vary, of course, by how much you have paid into the system (the report shows this) as well as how old you are when you collect your benefits. The Social Security Administration used to send these personalized reports in the mail, but now that they have gone paperless, they invite you to access their website and download the document.

In November 2015 Congress closed what some saw as two of the most lucrative filing loopholes: The file-and-suspend and restricted-spousal-application filing strategies. The speed with which the bill passed surprised both advisers and retirees. The changes will force many to change their retirement income plans.

Should I Take It at 62?

The earliest age at which you may begin drawing your Social Security benefits is 62. If you have reached that age and are now trying to decide whether to activate your benefits, you are not alone. But there are a few things you need to know before making this decision.

For one thing, you will be taking a reduced benefit if you opt to take it early. That reduction will not only affect you. If you are married, it may also affect your spouse. So you may want to give it some thought and resist the urge to choose impulsively. For most people, Social Security represents only a fraction of what they need to live on in retirement. But it is a valuable source of income that protects against three significant retirement risks – inflation, market volatility and longevity. It's guaranteed for life. It's one of the few income sources you can say that about.

Making the best decision about when to start Social Security can be complicated, particularly for married couples. And don't hold your breath waiting by the phone waiting for a representative of the federal government to call you up and give you advice on what to do. We apologize if that sounds flippant, but we are amazed at how many people seem to expect that to happen. The reality is, since Social Security is a federal benefit that you have earned, the government says that only you get to decide how to withdraw those earnings. So, while Social Security Administration people are usually very pleasant and are trained to know Social Security rules, they are actually prohibited from giving any personal advice. Their answers will be like the old "Dragnet" police show – "Just the facts, Ma'am." Even with all the facts, you will still have to decide on what strategy to follow to ensure you get the most out of the program. [18]

While we may not be able to give you advice, either, as financial advisers we can help you get educated about the myriad of options available to you when it comes to Social Security. If you ask us the "when" question, the answer will probably be "it depends." It really does depend. Each situation is different. If you have to take it because you need the money, then do so. Or if you are terminally ill, it makes no sense to wait. But if those two variables are not in play, every year you wait until age 70, the amount you stand to receive increases by approximately 8 percent. That's pretty hefty. Know anywhere else you can count on a guaranteed 8 percent rate of return?

Another advantage to working with a financial adviser to learn about your options is that we can show you how your Social Security decisions – when to begin withdrawals, whether to use your own record or your spouse's, etc. – may affect or be affected by the other pieces of your overall retirement income picture.

---

[18] William Meyer. ThinkAdvisor. Aug. 19, 2014. "Don't Take Retirement Advice From the Social Security Administration." http://www.thinkadvisor.com/2014/08/19/ dont-take-retirement-advice-from-the-social-security. Accessed Aug. 24, 2016.

In general, however, there are some "rules of thumb." You probably don't want to take your Social Security early IF:

- You are in good health, and your life expectancy is long.

- You are single, have very little savings and have a long life expectancy. Why? Because if Social Security is all you have, wait as long as possible to maximize your benefits.

- You plan on continuing to work, and you will earn more than the annual earnings limit before you reach full retirement age. Why? Social Security benefits are reduced if you earn more than the annual earnings limit.

- Your spouse is still working and has earned income that may cause more of your Social Security benefits to be taxed. Let's say your income and tax rate will be lower in a few years. If you wait, you can collect more and keep more of it.

- You are married, and your spouse's benefit is smaller than yours, and/or your spouse is much younger than you. Why? Because when you are married, your combined life expectancy will be longer than either single life expectancy. When you die, your spouse will continue to receive the larger of your Social Security benefit or their own, but not both. That means that if you take your Social Security at age 62, and your spouse's benefit is based upon your benefit, it will mean a reduced benefit for your surviving spouse's lifetime.

All that said, some we have met are just more comfortable having anything the government owes them in their hand. We understand that. We know of one man who has been very successful in life. He has built three businesses and sold each one of them for a hefty profit. He invested wisely, and he doesn't need the money. As soon as he turned 62, he signed up for his Social Security benefits because, as he puts it, this is his "knocking around money." You know what? More power to him! But for most of us, the decision is one that requires a little more thought.

Finding Good Advice

Before you make any decisions on Social Security, it would be wise to consult with a financial adviser who is competent in this area of retirement income planning. Firms like ours have access to computer programs that can help you make your decisions. These programs are designed to take data gathered from your Social Security statement, combine this with income needs and budget information, and give you specifics on how your decisions will affect you financially. If you ask your financial adviser specific questions about Social Security claiming options and you get a blank stare, you may want to get a second opinion!

Are you required to consult a financial adviser to make the best decisions about when to start your Social Security benefits? Of course not! You can study the information provided by the Social Security Administration. We find their website to be one of the best and most comprehensive sources of information. In fact, we were pleasantly surprised at how clearly presented the information was, especially compared to other sites we have seen administered by the government. But most people feel better getting professional input for this important decision – particularly if you need an adviser's help in other areas of retirement planning, such as how to use your retirement savings to generate reliable lifetime retirement income. If this is the case with you, consulting with a professional could be well worth your time and effort.

Baby Boomers Demographics

Social Security and Medicare

- Nearly 25% of boomers anticipate retiring at an age that does not make them eligible for full Social Security benefits; another 40 percent do not have a specific retirement age in mind.
- The annual cost-of-living adjustment (COLA) for Social Security payments was less than 3% for 14 of the past 20 years, including no increase in 2 of the past 3 years
- Social Security Administration officials predict the Social Security trust fund will go into the red in 2036. This is just 5 years after the youngest of the boomers will become eligible to receive full retirement benefits.
- Between 2036 and 2085, payroll taxes will be able to sustain only 3/4 of scheduled Social Security payments.
- Entitlement programs – Social Security, Medicare and Medicaid – represent 44% of non-interest federal spending. This level is expected to reach 60% 25 years from now.

(Sources: Office of Management and Budget, Social Security Administration, Insured Retirement Institute)

CHAPTER NINE

Solving the Long-Term-Care Dilemma

When the United States Department of Health and Human Services tells us that seven out of 10 people who live to the age of 65 will need some type of long-term care at some point in their lives, most Americans behave like ostriches. They metaphorically stick their heads in the sand, thinking maybe the problem will go away if they just don't look at it. But that doesn't change things. Typically, the biggest threat to our retirement nest eggs and our ability to maintain sufficient assets in the later years of our life is a life event that is health related, one for which we are unprepared.

Long-term care is the white elephant in the room that most folks don't want to admit exists. There is a lot of misunderstanding about long-term care: how much it costs, who pays for it, what public and private programs are available, and what is and isn't covered. So let's pull back the curtain and straighten a few things out, shall we?

Long-term care isn't cheap. There are several categories of long-term care. Assisted living facilities, adult day care, home health care and nursing home care are the four main ones. The cost of care varies by provider and by state and by the level of care needed. The 2014 Cost of Care Study by Genworth Insurance reveals that in the Phoenix-Mesa-Scottsdale area of Arizona, the average cost of a semi-private room in a nursing home is $71,996 per year. A private room will cost you $86,870 per year. The nationwide average is $77,380 for a semi-private room and $87,600 for a private room. According to the study, you can count on that cost increasing by around 4 percent over the next five years.

Medicare – Medicare does many things, but paying for long-term care is not one of them. Well, let us rephrase that. It pays for a smidgen. Medicare only pays for long-term care if you need skilled services or rehabilitative care in a nursing home but it will only cover 100 days. It's a stretch to say that is "long-term" care. Besides that, the average Medicare-covered stay is only 22 days. The key word here is "rehabilitative." Medicare doesn't cover the typical case of, for example, Alzheimer's patients who can no longer care for themselves. Don't look to Medicare to pick up the tab for non-skilled assistance with activities of daily living (ADLs), which make up the majority of long-term care services. The basic ADLs are bathing, dressing, eating, walking, grooming and toileting. Typically, when someone can't perform two out of six of those basic things, they are candidates for long-term care in a nursing home.

Medicaid – By some estimates, Medicaid pays for almost half of all long-term care in America. To qualify for Medicaid, however, you must officially be considered a pauper by the government. A note to those who think this is as easy as declaring yourself impoverished: The government won't just take your word for it. There is a gauntlet of qualifiers and myriad forms to fill out before you can qualify.

You will likely be dealing with a state government when it comes to qualifying for Medicaid. The program is funded at the federal level and administered by the states. The rules vary a bit from state to state, but they all require you to pay for it from your own assets or use private insurance first. Once that is exhausted, then you may apply for Medicaid, but you will have to meet strict minimum eligibility requirements in order to qualify.

It is common these days for individuals without long-term care insurance to attempt to protect their assets by adjusting their net worth before they become ill so they can qualify for Medicaid when the time comes. Getting rid of assets, perhaps giving them away to children, is one way to fit Medicaid criteria. This isn't illegal, but it's not easy to do. First of all, Uncle Sam knows it goes on and has put up a few roadblocks to discourage the practice. The main one is the "five-year look-back," an audit that is strictly imposed to prevent people from giving away their resources at the last minute just so they can qualify. Examiners look for anything of value you may have transferred out of your name, including even gifts of money earmarked for education. Unless you were paid full market value in return for any gifts, property or assets, the transfer will be disallowed, and the asset will be counted when calculating your Medicaid eligibility. This can get tricky. Some think that because the IRS allows you to gift up to $14,000 per year (as of 2014) to family, this is outside the scope of the Medicaid audit. Not so! It doesn't work to say, "Oops, I didn't know that," or "I forgot." Our recommendation is to seek the advice of an elder law attorney and a competent planning specialist when you are dealing with such matters. Many, it seems, are also not aware of the changes brought about by the Deficit Reduction Act of 2005 (DRA), which is when the current look-back period was changed from three years to five years.

Anyone who has been through this process will understand what "spend down" means. An applicant who is close to qualifying for Medicaid, but not there yet, must "spend down" his or her assets according to a list of items allowed. If the money is spent on items **not** on the "spend down" list, then the expenditure will be subject to the look-back. Approved "spend down" categories include pre-paying funeral expenses and replacing an automobile. The list is very specific.

Health care options are more limited for those on Medicaid as opposed to those who pay their own way or have insurance.

Traditional Long-Term-Care Insurance

The insurance industry began selling long-term-care insurance in the early 1980s, but as of 2010 relatively few have signed up for the coverage. The idea was for insurance companies to sell policies to people in their 50s and 60s so they would have the protection later if they needed it. The best time to buy traditional long-term care, or LTC, is, of course, when we are younger and have no health concerns. The longer you wait, the more expensive it is, and if you have health problems when you apply, you probably won't qualify. No insurance company wants to lose money on the deal.

The cost scares many away. For example, a person who is 60 might pay a minimum of $200 per month for a policy that provides $150 per day for a maximum of three years. Premiums and coverage vary, of course. That is just an example. But what if you pay all those premiums for decades and then die without ever needing the care? Is that money gone forever? Yes. Unless you pay for return-of-premium riders, traditional long-term care is a use-it-or-lose-it proposition. You build up no equity to pass on to any beneficiaries.

There is also no guarantee that your premium and your coverage will remain the same. What happens if you have a premium increase? You have four options: (a) pay the additional premium, (b) keep the premium the same by lowering your coverage amount, (c) keep the premium and the coverage amount the same by shortening the time of coverage or (d) stop paying the premiums and let the policy lapse. If you do the latter, however, all that money you paid in is gone.

LTC insurance is expensive as it is. The idea of it going up after you get it is disconcerting. Imagine buying a Mercedes for $10,000 down and $600 per month payments with a contract that allows the dealer to raise the monthly payments at will. A year goes by and you get a notice that your monthly payments have gone up to $700. You could take the car back, but you lose your down payment. That may sound like a ridiculous contract to sign, and yet that's what the traditional long-term care insurance contract says. It is easy to see why traditional LTC policies aren't exactly flying off the shelves. According to USAToday, only 8 million Americans own one. You might think that LTC policies are lucrative for the insurance companies, but not so. Many insurers have stopped selling them, and they have to plead with state regulators to raise rates on old policies.

So with all that on the table, there must be a better way to approach the problem.

Alternative LTC Coverage

Until recently, consumers had few choices when it came to long-term care health insurance. Traditional policies were all we had. But one thing is certain in a free enterprise economic system. If a profit-making organization – which is what an insurance company is – discovers a need they can fill at a profit, they will attempt to do so. Insurance companies put on their thinking caps and put their actuaries and product design people to work and came up with some inventive alternative approaches to cover long-term care needs. These new approaches are "hybrid" or "linked" policies. In insurance industry lingo they are called "combos" since they combine two distinct genres of insurance. For example, they may combine the benefits of an annuity or life insurance policy with certain aspects of a long-term care contract.

The one thing they wanted to ditch, however, was the use-it-or-lose-it feature.

With hybrid policies, you get, on the one hand, LTC benefits, or, if no LTC benefits are needed, you have, on the other hand, the insurance benefits for yourself and your beneficiaries

Life/LTC Hybrid

One policy links long-term care to a life insurance policy. With this plan, the insured deposits a set, single premium into a policy, creating an immediate pool of money. How much depends on the age, sex and health of the policyholder. This pool of money is either for long-term care or life insurance benefits. As an example, say a healthy 65-year old non-smoking female has $175,000 in liquid assets. If she deposits $50,000 into a policy like this, she would have approximately $87,000 in long-term-care benefits immediately. The life insurance component of the account would also provide a death benefit of around $87,000 for her beneficiaries. An optional rider is available, which she can purchase at an additional cost, and which would boost the long-term-care benefits to $260,000 (as opposed to the original $87,000). She has both a guarantee on her investment and protection from the high costs of a possible nursing home stay.

In another example, Pete buys a life insurance/LTC combination policy and pays a $50,000 premium for a $100,000 death benefit and a long-term care rider. The cash value (not the surrender value) is approximately $50,000. The long-term care benefit would be approximately $2,000 per month if needed. Keep in mind that any money paid out in long-term-care benefits reduces the policy's cash value by that same amount. The life/LTC combo is not for everyone, and not everyone can qualify. Health is definitely a factor. These hybrid policies have more options the younger you are. Why? Because at its base, this is a life insurance product and premiums for life insurance increase with age. The long-term-care benefit is usually around 2 percent of the death benefit. As with all life insurance, a physical is required.

Annuity Combo

Another of the new contracts gaining in popularity combines aspects of the traditional fixed annuity contract with long-term-care benefits. The annuity piece offers a guaranteed interest rate that is usually more than double what a bank would pay on a CD. The long-term-care piece pays out between two to three times whatever the value of the annuity happens to be at the time the care is needed and pays it out over a set period. Two or three years, say.

Say someone bought a $100,000 annuity/LTC hybrid contract. They might have a benefit limit of 300 percent – or a ceiling of $300,000 that could be spent for long-term care expenses. The coverage would last for two years, and the first $100,000 would come out of the annuity balance, followed by an additional $200,000, or up to that amount. Once the money runs out, the benefits end. Once the time of coverage expires, the benefits end.

What if you buy one of these combined policies and you die without ever needing long-term care? Then the product acts just like any other traditional fixed annuity. You can pass on the value to your heirs.

This is merely a broad-brush description of these products. The specific terms of the contract will vary from company to company. As with anything else, make sure you understand how these policies work before you buy one. They have a few moving parts and they are not for everybody. We suggest that you talk to an adviser who is up to date on these contracts. Health is a factor and there may be some underwriting involved. Just how much depends on the carrier. Another advantage to these new hybrid policies comes from the Protection Act of 2006. This legislation created a provision that makes premiums paid for LTC insurance tax free if they are paid from an annuity.

Not All Policies Are the Same

To summarize, with the life/LTC combo, either you use some or all of the LTC benefits or your heirs receive a life insurance payment. With the annuity/LTC combo, either you use some or all of the LTC benefits or you enjoy the proceeds of the annuity growth and then pass the remaining value of the contract along to your beneficiaries at death. These are much more appealing than the use-it-or-lose-it traditional LTC policies, especially for persons who are approaching retirement and have enough in the way of assets to invest. But they are a relatively new to the LTC planning landscape. Ask all the questions you can think of and then ask what questions you didn't think to ask to see if they are suitable for you.

Just as not all insurance companies are the same, not all combination policies are the same. Do your due diligence and check company ratings. Use ratings organizations such as A.M. Best, Moody's or and Standard & Poor's. Have your adviser do a benefits/premium analysis and compare the differences.

Miscellaneous Information about LTC

One reason most people don't educate themselves about long-term-care costs and coverage is because it is an unpleasant subject. We suppose it is the same reason life insurance salespeople have such a bad rap. They're always talking about death. Discussions on long-term care have to do with getting old and non-functional. Both are depressing subjects. So if you want to skip to the next chapter, go ahead. We won't hold it against you. But while we are here, we would like to pass along a few items that we found doing research for this book that we thought might be of interest to you.

Disqualifiers

Certain people can't qualify for long-term care coverage and this can be frustrating. Just as auto insurance is difficult to purchase if you have a troubled driving record, LTC insurance is denied to people with certain conditions. Standards vary between insurance companies, however. If one company denies you, another one may accept you. Here are some common reasons why you might not be able to buy LTC insurance:

- You are currently using long-term-care services.
- You already need help with the activities of daily living (ADLs) mentioned earlier – dressing, grooming, eating, bathing, walking and toileting.
- You have AIDS (acquired immunodeficiency syndrome) or AIDS-related complex (ARC).
- You have Alzheimer's disease or any form of dementia or cognitive dysfunction.
- You have a progressive neurological condition such as multiple sclerosis or Parkinson's disease.
- You had a stroke within the past year to two years, or a history of strokes.
- You have metastatic cancer (cancer that has spread beyond its original site).

It's like this: You have to not need the coverage before you can buy it. Put another way, if you are already in a position where you need the coverage, you probably can't buy it – even with asset-based LTC coverage. But the good thing is, once you do buy it, they have to cover you no matter what.

Things That Are Good to Know

The two main reasons you would purchase long-term care insurance of any kind is to (a) to protect your assets and (b) preserve your independence. There may be other places to look to cover this eventuality, especially if you are denied conventional coverage:

Reverse mortgages – These are home equity loans with a twist. They give you cash against the equity in your home and you are not required to sell the property. With most reverse mortgages, you may choose to receive a lump-sum payment to pay off any existing mortgage or other existing debts against your home. You can choose either a line of credit or a monthly payment. How you use the money is up to you and you get to continue living in the house. The deed stays in your name, and you must pay property taxes on the home and promise to keep it insured and in good repair. You don't have to repay the loan as long as you continue to live in the home. The amount you owe, based on loan payouts and interest on the loan, becomes due when you or the last borrower (usually the surviving spouse) dies, sells or permanently moves out of the home

To qualify for a reverse mortgage, you must be age 62 or older, and the loan must be on your primary residence. Unlike a traditional mortgage, you don't have to provide an income statement or show a good credit rating to get the loan.[19]

Life insurance options – Depending on the terms of the contract, you may be able to use your existing life insurance policy to help pay for long-term care services. We have already discussed the combination, or hybrid, products recently introduced. But there are other strategies that could work. One is the use of ***accelerated death benefits (ADBs).*** Some life insurance policies include a feature that allows you to receive a tax-free advance on your life insurance death benefit while you are still alive. Sometimes you must pay an extra premium to add this feature to your life insurance policy. Sometimes the insurance company includes it in the

[19] LongTermCare.gov. "Reverse Mortgages." http://longtermcare.gov/costs-how-to-pay/paying-privately/reverse-mortgages/. Accessed Aug. 24, 2016.

policy for little or no cost. There are different types of ADBs, each of which serves a different purpose. Depending on the type of policy you have, you may be able to receive a cash advance on your life insurance policy's death benefit if (a) you are terminally ill, (b) you have a life-threatening diagnosis such as AIDS, (c) you need long-term care services for an extended amount of time, or (d) you are permanently confined to a nursing home and incapable of performing certain ordinary activities of daily living (ADLs).

The amount of money you receive from these types of policies varies, but the accelerated benefit payment amount is usually capped at a certain percentage of the death benefit. Some policies, however, allow you to use the full amount of the death benefit. For ADB policies that cover long-term-care services, the monthly benefit you can use for nursing home care is typically equal to two percent of the life insurance policy's face value. The amount available for home care (if it is included in the policy) is typically half that amount. For example, if your life insurance policy's face value is $200,000, then the monthly payout available to you for care in a nursing home would be $4,000, but only $2,000 for home care. Some policies may pay the same monthly amount for care, regardless of where you receive the care. When you receive payments from an ADB policy while you are alive, the amount you receive is subtracted from the amount that will be paid to your beneficiaries when you die. ADB policy payouts for long-term care services are often more limited than the benefits you could receive from a typical long-term-care insurance policy. The face value of your life insurance policy may not be enough to allow ADB payments high enough to cover the actual cost of long-term care services you receive. The benefit payments may be too low, and the duration may be too short. But it's better than nothing.

If you want to leave an inheritance, you should consider whether using your life insurance death benefit to pay for long-term care services is the right option. If you use the ADB feature for long-term-care services, there may be little or no death benefit remaining for your survivors.

Life settlements – These plans allow you to sell your life insurance policy for its present value to raise cash for any reason. This option is usually only available to women age 74 and older and to men age 70 and older. You may choose to use the proceeds to pay for long-term care services. Some things to consider, however, are: (a) if you sell your life insurance policy, there may be little or no death benefit left for your heirs when you die, (b) the process does not require any health screens, which is a good thing if you are in ill health, and (c) the proceeds of the sale may be taxed.[20]

Viatical settlements – A viatical settlement is like a life settlement, but it is only possible if you are terminally ill. These plans allow you to sell your life insurance policy to a third party and use the money you receive to pay for long-term care. During the settlement process, a viatical company pays you a percentage of the death benefit on your life insurance policy, which is based not just on the value of the policy, but on your life expectancy. The viatical company then owns the policy and is the policy's beneficiary. The viatical company takes over payment of premiums on the policy and as a result receives the full death benefit after you die. Unlike the life settlement, money you receive from a viatical settlement is tax-free, if you have a life expectancy of two years or less or are chronically ill and the viatical company is licensed in the states in which it does business. You have to *prove* through medical records and a doctor's examination that you are terminally ill and have a life expectancy of two years or less in order to go this route, but this way there are no health requirements to satisfy for long-term health care insurance. Of course, if you use the viatical settlement option, your life insurance policy will not pay a death benefit to

---

[20] Long Term Care Online. "Alternatives to Long Term Care Insurance." http://www.longtermcareonline.com/alternatives.php. Accessed Aug. 24, 2016.

your heirs. Apparently, proving you qualify for a viatical is difficult; viatical companies approve less than half of all applicants.[21]

From a Planning Point of View...

When we are asked "Should I buy long-term care insurance?" we try to lay out the facts and the options and help the one asking the question make a well-informed decision. Like so many things, it would be easier if we knew the future. What we do know is that statistics show most people will need it at some point and you can only get insurance for something before it happens. To make an intelligent, informed decision you may wish to consider:

Your assets – You probably don't need $200,000 in collision insurance on your car if you drive a 10-year-old Toyota pickup truck. Let's face it: if you have very little in the way of assets, you have no investments and you don't own a home, getting Medicaid to pay for your long-term care is probably the best option. If, on the other hand, your assets are considerable and you can afford the premiums, why not buy the protection?

Your current health – If you battle obesity, hypertension, arthritis or if Alzheimer's runs in your family, you may wish to consider obtaining coverage. The longer you wait, the lower your chances will be of qualifying for LTC insurance.

Your age – The younger you are, the lower the premiums.

Admittedly, long-term care planning can be complicated and annoying. It's usually on the backside of Retirement Mountain. It's an area that presents itself for our concern on the down slope, the descent from the peak. We hope this information at least helps clear up some of the questions you may have had about the issue and has given you some useful information with which to confront the issue. Because there are so many options, so many decisions, it will benefit you to turn to a fiduciary, not an insurance

---

[21] Ibid.

product salesperson, to develop a strategy based on a thorough professional analysis of your unique situation.

CHAPTER TEN

The Need for Estate Planning Now

We saw a clever cartoon the other day. A snowman, complete with a carrot nose, top hat and sticks for arms, is standing under a bright sun and showing early signs of melting. That probably explains why the little pieces of coal that make the snowman's mouth form a downward arc. Beside the snowman is a man with a briefcase saying, "Mr. Frosty, it's March. Time to talk about estate planning."

Even though we push the thought of such an eventuality away most of the time, we are conscious that, someday, we will all meet the same fate as "Mr. Frosty" and melt away into the elements from whence we came. There are all kinds of euphemisms for death. Shakespeare's is the most colorful – "shuffle off this mortal coil." If you are a country music fan, there's the little quip Hank Williams sang, "I'll never get out of this world alive." Estate planning is one of those things we do out of love for our families. It's just the responsible and sensitive thing to do – make the communication of our final wishes and the transfer of our assets as streamlined and probate-proof as possible.

Avoiding Probate

Probate is like the traffic jam at the intersection of Last Will Drive and Testament Boulevard. It is not always a protracted legal mess that makes heirs frustrated and lawyers rich, but it can be if you either (a) don't do any estate planning or (b) do a poor job of it. Much of estate planning has to do with avoiding the snags of the probate process.

What is probate? There are two kinds of probate. Living probate is a court proceeding that occurs while you are alive. Death probate occurs at the time of your death. In general terms, probate is the legal process by which your assets are transferred to your heirs. The laws of the land dictate that the courts in each state govern the manner in which your fortune is distributed to those you leave behind.

"Even if I have a will?"

Yes, even if you have a will.

Probate can be time-consuming. The law of the land doesn't dictate that the court has to be in any particular hurry to make this transfer. It all depends on how complex the estate is and whether someone contests your posthumous instructions. A complicated estate that encounters contestants along the way can take years to settle. Attorneys become involved. Fees can accumulate, usually paid from the estate. Court proceedings are open to the public. Privacy is forfeited, and public scrutiny of your private affairs goes unchecked.

Probate Horror Stories

Want to hear a good probate horror story? Consider the case of Leona Helmsley, the hotel heiress who died in 2007 and left $12 million in a trust fund to Trouble, her tiny Maltese lapdog. You don't have to wonder what her two disinherited grandsons thought about that decision – it is all over the newspapers. The little dog was 12 at the time (that's 75 in dog years) and died in 2010, apparently from natural causes.

When she was alive, Helmsley, because she was a ruthless businesswoman with little tolerance for ineptitude, was called the "Queen of Mean." But that was just the opinion of people. We can only assume that she got along well with Trouble.

In 2008 a judge ruled that $12 million was much more than Trouble needed for her care and reduced her inheritance to $2 million. There is no record to indicate that the dog protested the ruling, so it stood. The only problem was when Trouble died she left no will. Not even a paw print! So the rest of the money in Trouble's trust went to charity. Can you imagine what the Helmsley grandkids thought of that?

Another estate planning mess was that of Michael Jackson, the "King of Pop." It wasn't that the one-glove-wearing superstar hadn't done any planning. He had. He just made some implausible choices that are still the subject of legal wrangling as this book is written. Jackson chose his aging mother to be the guardian of his children, with Diana Ross, the famous former member of the Motown singing group, The Supremes, as a backup guardian. The obvious question arose, what would happen if Jackson's mother died before his youngest child became an adult. Would the children have to uproot their lives with family to move in with Diana Ross?

Another problem with Jackson's estate was organization. He reportedly left so many investment accounts, bank accounts and documents scattered throughout the globe that getting a comprehensive snapshot of his entire estate was virtually impossible. The lesson here is to have an attorney pull your estate together for those you leave behind. Let trusted family members know where your important documents and assets are before you check out.

When Grateful Dead guitarist Jerry Garcia prepared his final papers, he named his third wife as executor of his estate, a move that didn't make his other family members very happy when they found out (after his death, of course). The lesson here is, while it is your right to choose who you wish to fulfill the role of executor of your estate, unless you just want to set off a firestorm when you die, give some thought to it. It may be better to name an unbiased person with the skills and credentials to orchestrate your affairs – such as an attorney – as your executor. The executor does not **need** to be an attorney necessarily, but legal expertise can certainly be helpful, especially if the estate has a degree of complexity to it.

Avoiding probate is one reason for getting the estate planning piece right before you die; another is inadvertently overpaying taxes. When James Gandolfini (star of the TV series, "The Sopranos") died, his will directed his executors to pay any estate taxes due on the entirety before his assets were divided up among his heirs. Liz Weston, writing in an article entitled, "Five Celebrities Who Messed up Their Wills," which appeared Aug. 1, 2013 in MSN Money, said, "The problem is that any wealth left to his wife, Deborah Lin, could have avoided estate taxes entirely. (Although the federal estate tax can kick in on estates worth more than $5 million, you can leave an unlimited amount to a spouse without incurring a tax bill.)"

Failure to update estate plans can lead to a probate nightmare. Take the case of Anna Nicole Smith. She was the *Playboy* centerfold who married elderly billionaire oil tycoon, J. Howard Marshall, who subsequently died. While she was fighting in probate court to claim the money Marshall had willed to her, she died. Her will left everything to her teenage son, who died shortly before she did. What a mess! To make matters worse, she had a baby days before the death of her son, only months before she herself died, yet never updated her estate plans to include the child. What lesson can we learn here? Update your wills regularly – reviewing at least once a year. When significant family events occur, such as divorces, marriages, births or deaths, re-structure your documents to accommodate them.

To Trust or Not to Trust

Estate planning, if done properly, is the final loving act we can perform for the benefit of our family and other loved ones to whom we wish to leave our worldly goods and fortune. We can see from the examples above that failure to plan properly in this regard can ensure a tangled mess for the ones we leave behind. Surely we can also agree that probate is like the proverbial banana peel on the sidewalk – something to sidestep if at all possible. But how? Well, it can be tricky, make no mistake. There are plenty of loopholes and pitfalls. You can avoid them, however, if you have the right financial advice from a fully trained, competent planning professional who has the proper credentials and training in the ins and outs of estate planning. This is certainly not a do-it-yourself zone. It is also an area where following errant advice can lead to grave mistakes. Take living trusts for example.

You can go online and obtain the forms for a **revocable living trust** (RLT) free of charge. It's a fill-in-the-blank affair that starts out: "I, (insert name), hereby transfer to (insert name) 'trustee', the property set forth on Schedule A attached hereto and made a part hereof, to be held IN TRUST, for the purposes of and in accordance with the provisions which follow:"

Some think that when they buy these documents and fill in the blanks they are home free when it comes to estate planning, and nothing could be further from the truth. Some who promote living trusts as the end-all-be-all of probate avoidance suggest that when you transfer your assets to the living trust and make yourself (or yourself and your spouse) the trustees of that trust, you can have your cake and eat it too. After all, it is a *revocable* trust. You can change or cancel it at any time. While you are living, nothing has really changed. Your assets technically don't belong to you; they belong to the trust. But since you are the trustee you have full control over them and when you die, the trust ensures that your assets go automatically to your heirs without having to slog through probate. Not only that, but you saved thousands of dollars in attorney fees! We have seen some advertisements that claim that RLTs can save you thousands of dollars in estate taxes. It would be wonderful if all this were true, but it isn't. In most cases RLTs offer you about as much tax protection as a will, the key word being "revocable." If you can change it at any time, as the name implies, the tax laws still recognize you as the owner of those assets. From a tax standpoint, property owned inside the trust is viewed the same as if it were outside of it. Don't believe the myth that RLTs stop the taxman dead in his tracks. That is a common misconception that has gotten plenty of grantors into trouble. The IRS has even been known to discriminate even against such trusts in certain income tax scenarios, viewing them as a tax dodge. Our experience is that the government will always find a way to get what they are legally owed, and an RLT does not legally exempt you from paying taxes.

We are not saying that RLTs aren't worthwhile estate planning tools; they are. They are just not the invisible, bullet-proof shield some make them out to be. There are situations where they apply, but we often see situations where other options are better. There are always going to be advantages and disadvantages to every financial tool you use to plan your retirement. Revocable trusts are typically very rigid, not allowing for flexibility when it would be desirable, say, in the event of a sudden death or disability involving the trustee. A married couple, for example, doesn't need an RLT to avoid probate if they can own their assets jointly with rights of survivorship.

Did you know that every single dollar in a living trust is open and exposed to being seized by nursing homes and Medicaid if you become ill enough to require round-the-clock skilled nursing care? A living trust is designed to avoid probate so that your **heirs** don't have to go through the lawyers and the legal fees. The trust isn't for you; it's for those you leave behind.

Where an RLT Can Come in Handy

A revocable living trust is created when the person granting the trust signs an agreement that designates a person or a company to take control of a trust. Sometimes the trustee and the grantor are the same person. When this is the case, it is a good idea to appoint a co-trustee to ensure that the administration of the estate stays in the right hands in case the trustee dies or becomes incapacitated. When the grantor names a corporate administrator as trustee, the estate will likely remain in competent hands, but it could cost a fortune, too.

A revocable trust can be an effective way to continue managing one's estate during disability. Your property remains available to you and is used for your benefit even if you are not physically or mentally capable of administering your affairs.

Revocable trusts are also flexible. You can name whomever you want to be the primary administrator of your property, and it is relatively easy to make amendments if you deem it necessary. Of course, the primary benefit of a revocable trust is the avoidance of probate, and that can be of greater or lesser importance to you depending on the complexity of your estate. For example, if you own property in more than one state, an RLT may be just what you need to avoid multiple probate hearings. We still recommend that you obtain local legal counsel in these situations.

A revocable trust doesn't always "auto-adapt" when your circumstances change. In most jurisdictions, if structured properly, the provisions of a will change automatically upon marriage, divorce and the birth of a child. Revocable trusts usually don't retain this flexibility. It is up to the grantor to make necessary amendments to the provisions in an RLT. If he or she does not do so, the assets in the trust could wind up in the wrong hands.

The best thing to do is find the estate planning solution that is custom fitted to your unique financial and family situation. A misstep here could put property and assets in jeopardy.

What a Living Trust WON'T do

Living trusts are fine, but the estate planning road does not end there. Some reason this way: "Our lawyer put together a family living trust. We've got annuities in there, the stocks, the IRAs and the 401(k) plans. We're *all set!*" Not really. That living trust will not reduce the taxes you owe to Uncle Sam each and every year. It won't reduce your exposure to market risk. It won't increase the low returns your brokerage accounts produce, nor will it reduce the fees and expenses inside those accounts, even if you have them titled to your trust. Your living trust will not help you with your IRA taxes. If you were considering stretching the distributions from your IRA over the lives of your beneficiaries, keep in mind that the government-required minimum distributions are based on the age of your beneficiaries. If your beneficiary is your trust, what age is it? Typically, when a trust is the beneficiary of an IRA, your IRA must pay out immediately on your death, triggering a significant tax event on your hard-saved assets. Your living trust will also not protect one single dollar from a catastrophic lawsuit. Nor will it help you if you should wind up with a catastrophic illness with limited or no insurance.

The Case for Living Wills

Death and dying are normally not favorite topics of discussion when families get together. But everyone knows the old saying about death and taxes. Preparing for the inevitable is part of estate planning, and it is probably one of the most loving things one can do for those they leave behind. It does not have to be a cold and detached affair. It can be viewed as a celebration of life and ensuring that future generations will benefit from decisions you make today.

Living wills and advance medical directives spell out your specific instructions regarding health care and end-of-life decisions. These documents express your preferences and relieve your loved ones from all the hand-wringing that goes along with such matters. Once these documents are in place, a health care power of attorney should be signed so your loved ones know clearly who has the responsibility to instruct doctors and nurses as to what to do. These decisions are made when you are alert and cognizant of your surroundings so that, if there comes a time when you are unable to communicate your wishes, perhaps due to unconsciousness or a terminal illness, others will know exactly what to do. Some wish to avoid artificial life support. Others may want to be kept alive as long as humanly possible. Either way, these documents speak for you if you can no longer speak for yourself.

Over the years, newspapers have been full of the unfortunate stories where people in a coma, for example, have been at the center of a family controversy where sons, daughters and spouses are left to air out their passionate opinions before insatiable reporters. Who can forget the case of Terri Schiavo of Petersburg, Florida? In 1990, she collapsed and was rushed to the hospital. She remained in a coma for the next eight years, kept alive by machines. The doctors gave her no hope of ever regaining meaningful awareness. When her husband finally decided to have her feeding tube removed, which would end her life, her parents fought the move. The bitter struggle with Terri at the center dragged through the courts for years while the question echoed, "What would Terri have wanted?" A living will would have answered that question and settled the issue quickly, sparing all the anguish. Health care professionals respect these documents and are relieved when families have them. Most who don't have these documents in place procrastinate because they surmise such things are for the sick and elderly. Not true. Anyone could have an accident or a sudden illness.

Power of Attorney

John and Martha are on a road trip and they have a tragic car accident. They survive, badly injured. The good news is they will recover. The bad news is it will require them to be hospitalized for six months or perhaps more. Who is going to make sure the ordinary things of life are cared for? It's winter. Who will pay the utility bills so the heat stays on and the pipes don't freeze? Hopefully, John and Martha have appointed someone they trust to act on their behalf, perhaps a daughter or son, and given them a durable power of attorney. Such a document should be included in your estate plan, and a copy kept with your estate planner or your attorney, with another copy kept in a fire-proof safe in your home.

Updating Beneficiaries

Designated beneficiaries for IRAs, annuities and life insurance policies take precedence over any provision in a last will and testament. It is crucial that you update these regularly and especially if life events occur that produce a change in family relationships.

We do a three-step review with new clients and examine all documents that contain a designated beneficiary line. We find that some are blank. We find that others have listed a lending institution or a financial adviser as the beneficiary. Since beneficiary designations are incontestable, the name listed on the document is the person to whom the money goes, regardless of any protest or logical rendering of circumstances that have presented themselves after the fact.

In one case, a man who had not updated his documents inadvertently left his former wife as the sole beneficiary on his $2 million life insurance policy when he remarried. Upon the man's death, his widow was left penniless while his former wife enjoyed the proceeds from the policy. There was nothing anyone could do about the situation except offer a whistle and a shake of the head.

CHAPTER ELEVEN

Using Insurance to Fund a Tax-Free Retirement - Say What?

'Truth is stranger than fiction, but it is because fiction is obliged to stick to possibilities; Truth isn't." – Mark Twain

Whenever the word "insurance" comes up, reactions range from eye-rolling to, "Ugh, can we just skip this part?" For some, insurance ranks at the top of the "necessary evil" list. "It's better to have it and not need it than to need it and not have it," as the old saying about insurance goes.

Have you ever noticed to what lengths the carriers go to make us think warm and fuzzy thoughts about insurance? They have mascots for pitchmen. MetLife has Snoopy. Geico has the cute little gecko. Aflac has the comedic duck. It's the spoonful of sugar that makes the medicine go down.

Insurance insulates us from the uncertainties of life. If you own a home, you have insurance to cover the financial loss you would incur should your home be destroyed by fire or damaged by a storm. If you own a car, you realize the financial responsibility you bear, and you buy insurance to cover it. No one wants to dwell on tragedy, but we all know it could strike at any time, and insurance is a guarantee that we will be made financially whole should the unforeseen occur.

The Origin of Life Insurance

Humans have yet to figure out a way to keep from dying. It is the one eventuality upon which we can all depend. Our lives are affected by death, even if it is the passing of a loved one. Life insurance was "invented" to help us cope with the financial side of that eventuality. According to the Insurance Barometer Study by LIMRA, an insurance research organization, 70 percent of people age 65 and older own at least one life insurance policy.[22]

The whole thing started with the ancient Romans, who gave us other world-changers, such as concrete and the aqueduct. Around 100 B.C., soldiers in one of the companies of the Roman Legion formed a "burial club" for their families. The club would pay for the funeral rites and burial of fallen soldiers. Soldiers pooled their resources, thus making it possible for all soldiers, rich or poor, to participate. It was the first recorded incidence of "resource pooling." Romans believed that without a ceremonial burial, the dead would become unhappy and haunt their loved ones. The "burial club" idea gradually spread to other military camps and was soon routine.

The idea of insurance, or "risk pooling," to cover burial expenses was gradually embraced by the Roman population at large but remained limited to families and fraternal groups. When the ancient Roman civilization fell, the idea of insurance went with it. Centuries would pass before the idea was picked up again in 17th century England.

---

[22] Ashley Durham. LIMRA. 2015. "2015 Insurance Barometer Study." http://www.orgcorp.com/wp-content/uploads/2015-Insurance-Barometer.pdf. Accessed Dec. 13, 2016.

It was England's Sir Edmund Halley who made commercial insurance as we know it today possible. Wait, the comet guy? Yes, the comet guy. Halley was one of those renaissance men we learned all about in high school. He was a colleague of Sir Isaac Newton. While not quite the math genius that Newton was, Halley was destined for great things from a young age. Halley's father was a wealthy man and was able to send young Edmund to Oxford University where he became a master astronomer and developed a love of mathematics.

Edmund Halley Sr. had just gone through a disastrous marriage that depleted most of his resources. This, of course, dried up some of the financial support the now-famous Edmund Jr. had received from his father. Things got worse. In March 1684 Edmund Halley Sr. disappeared and was found dead five weeks later. His death is still a mystery. While administering his father's estate, Halley stumbled upon an idea that would change history. He became curious about the statistical mortality of humans. When he wasn't peering at the stars through the lens of a telescope, Halley was hunched over a desk working on actuary tables that would eventually pave the way for insurance premiums.

Halley's search for data led him to, of all places, the Polish city of Breslau (now Wroclaw) where, for some reason, the city fathers kept meticulous records of when its citizens were born, when they died, as well as to details about their lives. Halley took that information and published an article in 1693 entitled *"An Estimate of the Degrees of the Mortality of Mankind."* In it, Halley didn't just go into detail about his findings, he wrote out the mathematical formula that insurance companies would use over the next three centuries to determine the appropriate premiums to charge for certain ages for life insurance.[23]

---

[23] Cerebro.xu.edu. "Edmund Halley." http://cerebro.xu.edu/math/Sources/Halley/halley.html. Accessed Aug. 24, 2016.

Why We Have Life Insurance

The fundamental reasons for owning life insurance haven't changed much since the 17th century or the days of ancient Rome.

- **Providing for our families:** When we are young, we own life insurance to replace the incomes upon which others depend. The least expensive is term life insurance. Term life, as the name implies, covers the insured for a specified period – 10, 20 or 30 years. The older we get, the higher the premiums. Essentially, insurance companies are betting we will live to full life expectancy and hopefully outlive the policy. The insurance runs out (or gets too expensive for us to renew), and they come out ahead. We pay the inexpensive premiums hoping we won't collect. Whole life (or permanent life) insurance costs more to own, but it never runs out. These types of policies have a cash value element which grows over time. When we are older, we own life insurance to cover such things as estate taxes, funeral costs or leaving our heirs a legacy.

- **Funeral costs:** The average funeral costs about $6,000, with an additional $3,000 for the vault, liner and gravesite. Cremation? Around $3,700. Preplanned funerals prepaid with designated life insurance proceeds are becoming more and more popular. Preplanning our final arrangements makes it easier on our heirs both financially and emotionally. They just follow the checklist and have the peace of mind that our wishes were honored.

- **Planned giving:** Policies are often purchased as our "going-away present" to our favorite university, church or other charity. We may also purchase life insurance to take care of organizations that took care of us, perhaps leaving funds behind that will help them carry on a work that we support.

- **College funds:** Paying for a college education can be a burden to working parents. Life insurance can be used to offset this—from borrowing against an overfunded policy to using a parent or grandparent's death benefits. According to the College Board,[24] the average cost of one year of college (tuition and board) is about $11,438 for community college, $19,548 for a public university in your home state and $43,921 for a private university. Is it worth that much? It is according to a 2014 Pew Research Center report, which claims that, on average, those with college degrees earn $17,500 more per year than those without one.

- **Taxes:** Life insurance proceeds can take care of federal estate taxes and state inheritance taxes. This makes it possible for heirs to keep the bulk of their inheritance instead of forking a sizable portion of it to the taxman.

- **Funding a tax-free retirement:** Yes, you read correctly. Life insurance can be used to produce an income for retirement that is completely tax-free. Not tax-deferred ... tax-free. If you aren't familiar with the concept, please allow us to provide a little background on how and why it came into existence.

The Insurance Revolution

In the early 1980s, an insurance revolution of sorts took place in America. Inflation seemed out of control in the late 1970s and early 1980s. Interest rates climbed as high as 18 percent. Baby boomers were just starting to come of age as responsible citizens with jobs, mortgages and insurance and started to wonder why insurance companies were paying only 1 or 2 percent interest on the cash value portion of their whole life insurance policies when the banks were paying double-digit interest on CDs. Financial times were changing, and insurance companies were stuck in the 1950s, paying an arbitrary low percentage of interest as they had done for years. Insurance companies were not legally required to

---

[24] College Board. 2015. "Trends in Higher Education Series: Trends in College Pricing 2015." http://trends.collegeboard.org/sites/default/files/2015-trends-college-pricing-final-508.pdf. Accessed Dec. 6, 2016.

disclose all the details of the inner workings of the policy to policy owners; so they didn't. It wasn't until consumers started cashing out their whole life policies by the droves, investing their cash at higher returns, and buying cheaper term life policies to replace death benefits that insurance company executives began to see a need to retool. Now forced to compete, insurance companies put their actuaries and product-design people to work and came up with a new concept – investment-grade life insurance. It would bear the name universal life (UL) because of its flexibility and transparency. Interest on cash value policies would no longer be arbitrary but would be pegged to U.S. Treasury bills. In 1982, T-bills were paying an attractive 14.59 percent! This was public knowledge. Policy owners could keep track of their returns on a daily basis if they wished. UL premiums were quite flexible, too. Consumers had the option to pay more into the policy during feast and pay less or even skip premiums during famine. Death benefits remained tax free, and policy holders could even make withdrawals in the form of low-interest loans. It must be noted that part of this new openness was because insurance companies realized it made for better customer relations, and part of it was the result of new legislation by Congress requiring a higher level of transparency. At first, there was no limit on how much an investor could pump into these policies. Keep in mind, the cash value grew tax deferred and could be removed tax free. Who was left out of that picture? Uncle Sam! Soon, new IRS laws appeared that limited the amount you could invest in IUL policies. The Tax, Equity, Fiscal and Responsibility Act (TEFRA) passed in 1982. This was followed two years later by DEFRA, the Deficit Reduction Act and in 1988, the last of the regulatory triplets, TAMRA, or Technical and Miscellaneous Revenue Act was born.

When Treasury bill rates began to taper off, a few of the larger insurance companies went back to the drawing board and, in 1997, introduced *indexed universal life.* It was a variation on the same theme, but this time with a brand new method of crediting interest to cash value life policies. These new policies pegged returns to the upward movement of a stock market index, such as the S&P 500, while retaining such desirable characteristics as flexibility of premiums and an adjustable face value (death benefit). Policyholders could juice up the earning capacity of the policy by "overfunding," that is, pouring more into the policy than was required to provide the maximum death benefit. The aforementioned regulations of the 80s curbed abuse of the tax-free provisions, and there were limits on your contributions, but with these new investment-grade life policies, individuals could now benefit from a surging stock market without the downside risk! Finally, life insurance product owners were able to benefit from bull (rising) markets while remaining protected from bear markets when share prices fell.

A Look "Under the Hood" of IUL

How were these new investment-grade insurance concepts received? According to LIMRA, an insurance research organization, IULs are the fastest-growing type of life insurance on the market. Sales of the product grew by 549 percent from 2006 to 2015.[25, 26] It behooves us to take a look at the inner workings of this high-powered instrument before considering it as an option for retirement income. Among the characteristics of IUL are the following:

- **Guaranteed principal AND guaranteed gains:** IUL policies are designed with a built-in ratchet/reset feature that allows your cash value to benefit from the gains of a

---

[25] Frank Howell. LifeHealthPro. Feb. 1, 2008. "The Coming of Age of Index Universal Life." http://www.lifehealthpro.com/2008/02/01/the-coming-of-age-of-index-universal-life. Accessed Dec. 6, 2016.

[26] Cyril Tuohy. Insurance News Net. March 16, 2016. "Indexed Annuities, Indexed Life Sales Hit Record Highs." http://insurancenewsnet.com/innarticle/indexed-annuities-indexed-life-post-sales-records. Accessed Dec. 6, 2016.

stock market index, lock in those gains and remain immune to market losses. The crash of 2008 was an example of a time that policyholders benefitted from this feature. While they made modest gains during some of the steep upward motion of the stock market in the years immediately preceding, policyholders lost nary a dime when the stock market plummeted.

- **Tax-free death benefit:** Your named beneficiary will be paid the death benefit from your IUL policy in tax-free dollars.

- **Cash flow for retirement is tax free:** Because of the low-interest loan provision, policyholders may have access to a source of income that is free of state and federal taxes.

Moving Parts

Looking at the inner workings of indexed universal life reminds us of what lies under the hood of a modern, high-powered automobile. There are quite a few moving parts and it is easier to describe what these policies do than how they do it. That's why they are sometimes called investment-grade life insurance policies or "advanced" life policies. But if you work with professional advisers who are certified and fully trained, they should be able to answer all your questions satisfactorily.

How they work is essentially as follows: When you pay a premium into an IUL, part of the premium pays for insurance (annual renewable term coverage) based on the life of the one being insured. This part is funded first. What is left over is added to the policy's cash value. That is why people using an IUL for a tax-free retirement will "overfund" the policy, thus accelerating the cash growth. The cash value is credited with interest based on the upward movement of a stock market index, such as the S&P 500, the Nasdaq, the Dow or a combination of these. You are not invested directly in the market. That's why the gains lock in, and you don't lose when the market goes down. IULs typically offer a guaranteed minimum fixed interest rate and allow the policyholder to choose what percentage he or she wants to be pegged to the fixed interest and what percentage pegged to the index.

Simply stated, the cash value goes up when the market index goes up and remains unchanged when the market goes down. There are detailed fine-tuning adjustments within that framework that your adviser can help you make. Typically, interest is credited to the cash account once per year. Some bullet points you need to know if you are considering this strategy for your retirement are:

- Cash values grow tax deferred, not tax free. If you let the policy lapse prematurely, you may create a taxable event.
- The cash value can be used to pay the insurance premiums if necessary.
- There are caps on how the percentage of stock market index growth is credited to your account. In other words, the index may skyrocket up 30 percent in a year, and your cap may only allow 15 percent credited to your cash value.
- The death benefit is permanent and completely tax free. When you make withdrawals from the cash value of the policy, this may reduce the death benefit by the same amount.
- Larger face amounts are better if you intend to use these policies for cash accumulation.
- The younger you are, the more horsepower you have for cash accumulation with these policies. Why? Because less of your premium is used to pay for the death benefit.
- Even though you may be using life insurance to produce tax-free living benefits, it is still life insurance. You must be healthy enough to qualify for coverage, and you will likely be required to take a medical exam before your application is approved.

What Ed Slott Says

Ed Slott, who is probably one of America's most well-respected authorities on retirement income planning in general and IRAs in particular, has become a regular on National Public Television. His opinions are forthright and free of bias. In one televised appearance, he said the following about indexed universal life:

> "As a tax adviser, I'm advising you to take advantage of the single biggest benefit in the tax code, and that is the tax exemption for life insurance... Most people think of life insurance as something that pays off after you're dead. That's true! But what if I told you that you can have tax-free access to your life insurance during your lifetime? You could use it for yourself. You could be moving large amounts of money from taxable accounts to a tax-free permanent life insurance policy where the money grows tax-free inside the policy."

Slott acknowledges that the government controls the amount investors can put into IUL, but says this might be an area where you want to put the maximum you can into the policy.

"If you are approaching retirement or already retired and looking to shelter more of your taxable money into a tax-free vehicle, this might be the place for you," Slott said. "Why would you keep money growing in a taxable account when it could be transferred to a tax-free investment? If you have taxable IRA funds, you can, in effect, convert your IRA to life insurance."

The way Slott sees it, paying tax now at low rates on distributions from your IRA, and then using that money to fund your life insurance investment accomplishes two things: (a) reducing future tax exposure in your IRA by taking distributions now and (b) building up a tax-free source of retirement funds should you need them.

"If it turns out that you don't need to tap into your life insurance investment for retirement income," Slott says, "then the life insurance benefit builds for your family, income tax free. And for most people, it will be estate tax free, too, depending on the estate tax exemption level."

IUL policies are not for everyone. As with any financial product, they must fit you and they must fit your overall wealth management strategy. We agree with Ed Slott they have many benefits and features that are worth checking into.

How Safe Are Insurance Products?

The law requires insurance companies to maintain reserves equal to 100 percent of their liabilities. That is the main spar in the safety underpinnings of insurance companies. The government also regulates how those reserves are invested.

In 2013, the CIPR (Center for Insurance Policy and Research) released "Study on the State of the Life Insurance Industry." The study concluded that during the 10 years of economic turmoil between 2002 and 2012, the life insurance industry "significantly outperformed the banking industry."

Historically, banks have failed while insurance companies survived. The CIPR research concluded that only 20 out of 350 insurers (5.7 percent) went into receivership during the Great Depression. Of those that failed, virtually all of the policyholder claims were still honored by solvent reinsurers. On the other hand, more than 4,000 state and national banks failed in 1933 at the height of the Great Depression, and depositors lost about $1.3 billion.

CHAPTER TWELVE

Advisers and Brokers Are Not One and the Same

On the morning of May 13, 2012, in New Delhi, India, Kamini Solanki, a pregnant schoolteacher, woke up with a fever and complained of pain throughout her body. Her husband drove her to the office of her "gynecologist," who, upon a brief examination, recommended she check into the hospital immediately. The anxious couple waited for eight hours while her condition worsened. Kamini died later that night of septicemia, a blood infection that, if not treated promptly, is always fatal. Her husband later discovered that the gynecologist had only a bachelor's degree in medicine and that the hospital "doctor" had no medical training at all.

The widowed husband sued and an investigation revealed more than 40,000 "doctors" were practicing medicine in India without qualifications and certification.[27]

---

[27] India Today. Nov. 4, 2015. "DMC suspends 4 doctors for negligence in duty." http://indiatoday.intoday.in/story/dmc-suspends-4-doctors-for-negligence-in-duty/1/516154.html. Accessed Aug. 24, 2016.

It pays to do a background check on anyone who is going to slice you open. Consider the case of Lucas Ebert, who for years pretended to be a plastic surgeon at Oregon Health and Science University Hospital until his bogus diagnoses and botched surgeries caught up with him in 2011. One woman treated by Ebert will be in a wheelchair for the rest of her life. Ebert was exposed and sentenced to three years in prison.[28]

Those are extreme and rare cases of misplaced trust in fraudulent professionals, of course. Most medical professionals are who they say they are and are not con artists or mentally disturbed individuals who get a thrill out of pretending to be doctors. The same is true of the financial profession. But it is relatively easy to hang out a shingle and claim that you are a "financial professional," even if you have no SEC certification and are limited to just the few financial products your company allows you to sell. These folks are not necessarily ill-intentioned, but their advice can be just as bad for your wealth as advice from an ill-trained doctor can be for your health.

Fiduciaries vs. Suitability Advice

The term "fiduciary" is not a word we use in everyday conversation. In fact, you could probably go the entire year without using it in a sentence. But if you are seeking professional advice on money matters, it is a word we should fully understand. Here's what the dictionary says:

Fiduciary: [fi-doo-shee-er-ee] noun. Law. A person to whom property or power is entrusted for the benefit of another.

We are fiduciaries because that is the legal and ethical relationship we have with our clients. The word "fiduciary" legally defines

---

[28] Aimee Green. The Oregonian. Dec. 23, 2011. "Lucas Ebert, who pretended to be OHSU doctor and businessman, gets 3 years in prison." http://www.oregonlive.com/portland/index.ssf/2011/12/young_man_who_pretended_to_be.html. Accessed Aug. 24, 2016.

the relationship between a client and any professional where the interests of the client are **always** put first, regardless of any other consideration.

The world of investment counseling can be broken down into two camps – those who adhere to the **suitability standard** and those who adhere to the **fiduciary standard.** You may have never heard of either of these standards, and you aren't alone. In 2011, the U.S. Securities and Exchange Commission conducted a study that found "many investors are confused by the standards of care that apply to investment advisers and broker-dealers."

Suitability is the lesser of these two standards. For example, a broker may recommend an investment if it is "suitable" to you. Suitable, that is, for your age, investment goals and objectives, and personal risk-tolerance threshold. But if there is more than one investment that fits your needs, the broker is within his legal rights to recommend the one that will offer him or her the highest commission. Technically, this is ethical and legal, according to the legal standard of suitability.

Registered Investment Advisers and Investment Adviser Representatives such as ourselves, however, stay within the guidelines of the higher **fiduciary** standard, which keeps us bound by law to offer only what is in the best interests of each client. Earning a higher commission based on what we offer a client is never a consideration.

You may be wondering where the fiduciary standard came from. It was established as part of the Investment Advisers Act of 1940 and is regulated by the Securities and Exchange Commission, or state securities regulators.

The term "fiduciary" comes from the Latin word "fidere," which means "trust." A fiduciary is legally and ethically bound to make investment recommendations that are not merely suitable, but are in the client's best interest. When there is a conflict of interest, fiduciaries are to put client interests ahead of their own. In some other commercial settings, you pay extra for better service – an upgrade from coach to first class on an airline, or a private hospital room, for example – but you pay nothing extra for fiduciary advice. That doesn't mean a fiduciary is not compensated monetarily for his or her services, it just means they are not *motivated* by profit.

How do you know if you're hiring a fiduciary? The easiest way is the most obvious. Just ask! In fact, ask this exact question: Are you acting under the fiduciary or suitable standard? If the answer is "fiduciary," ask them to put it in writing.

So what's wrong with a *suitability* standard? The word "suitability" itself is one that carries a positive connotation. You would think that, logically, any advice deemed suitable is clearly in your best interests. In the financial world, however, suitability leaves the door open to the possibility of a conflict of interests. An investment broker's duty is to the broker-dealer he or she works for first, not the client. The need to disclose potential conflicts of interest is not a requirement for brokers.

Please understand that we do not believe that all investment brokers are unethical or are taking unfair advantage of their clients. Quite the opposite is true. Most broker-dealers are ethical, in our estimation. It's just that fiduciary financial advisers do not work for a large brokerage house. They are not confined to a sales "menu" provided them by a corporation. They can recommend any number of strategies and approaches they feel best equip their clients to accomplish their financial goals. Fiduciary financial advisers are legally and ethically bound to provide full disclosure and work solely in the interests of their clients while most brokers are not.

Doing the Right Thing

There is nothing wrong with asking how your financial adviser gets paid for his or her services. Most would initially think it rude to ask such a bold question, but this is different. This is about your money. You are **trusting** someone with what is, perhaps, your life's savings. If there is a conflict of interests when it comes to your money, you need to know about it ASAP!

There is nothing inherently wrong with anyone earning commissions. Maybe you've used a travel agency to plan a vacation before. They often provide excellent service and can save you lots of money because they can shop for the best value on accommodations and travel fares. These people are compensated by the airlines and the hotels. We don't have a problem with it because we were able to benefit by their knowledge and expertise and the network of providers at their fingertips. Of course, it would be another matter if the travel agent booked a flight for you on a non-competitive airline, or put you up in a seedy hotel, just because there was a higher commission in it for the agent.

If you are talking to an adviser that doesn't seem forthcoming or willing to answer your questions quickly and clearly, it is almost always an indication that you need to look elsewhere.

Taking Ownership of Your Finances

Sometime after suffering through the market meltdown of 2008, Harold and Bonnie came to our office. They were upset. As we listened to their story, it wasn't hard to understand why. Both of them were 62 years old and jointly owned and operated a florist shop in downtown Scottsdale that had serviced the community for over 20 years. Like most businesses, they had started small and grew quite successful as the area blossomed. They loved their business. For over two decades, Harold and Bonnie went out of their way to make sure their customers were happy and satisfied. They took it personally if a customer wasn't ecstatic, especially Bonnie.

As is often the case, they were so wrapped up in making the business successful that they neglected to look after the money it generated. Most of the money the business made was put right back into the business. They called it "re-seeding." The good news was the business was debt free and earning a profit. The bad news was that the rest of their money was placed in the hands of a financial advisory firm that they had trusted confidently.

The couple was on a first name basis with the people who worked at the firm and it never really occurred to them to question the advice they received. As long as the numbers were up, Harold would usually just open the statements from their broker and file them away.

They had plans to retire at age 65, sign the shop over to their competent children, and tour the country in a recreational vehicle that was yet to be purchased. Running a successful business had afforded them no time for vacations in past 20 years. They figured they would make up for lost time when they retired. Bonnie had a map on which she had highlighted the "blue highways," or secondary highways, they intended to travel. She kept the map in a folder with brochures on several places they intended to visit once they retired.

When the market crashed in 2008, they lost over half their nest egg and their retirement plans evaporated like dandelion spores in a stiff breeze. The broker said he was sorry, but there was nothing anyone could do. The money was just gone. They were told to "hang in there."

We were able to help stop the bleeding and put them back on solid ground with what remained of their portfolio. Unfortunately, there was no way to avoid the fact that they would have to work another three years past their retirement goal.

"I wish we had paid more attention," said Bonnie.

Of course, she was right. They both should have been paying more attention. While a certain amount of trust in your adviser is a good thing, blind trust is not. You should always know where your assets are and why they are there. Ask questions. Ask more questions. Ask until you completely understand the investment strategies that you are being presented. And please read the fine print. We've all heard the old axiom, "The devil is in the details." You are the admiral of the fleet. Nobody else will care as much about your financial well-being as you.

Choosing the Right Financial Adviser for *YOU*

You've heard the old saying, "different strokes for different folks." That applies in choosing the right financial adviser. Just as medical professionals specialize, so do financial advisers. Some specialize in accumulation. The young, working years when you are earning a living and saving and investing for the future. Others specialize in asset preservation and distribution. These are the later years in life when you are approaching retirement. The advice that got you to the golden years is most often not the advice that will get you **through** the golden years. Conservative investing is called for. You don't want to lose what you have worked all those years to acquire. You want your resources to (a) continue working for you and earning a reasonable rate of return, and (b) last for the rest of your life.

When you reach adulthood, you don't go see your pediatrician for medical advice. While your pediatrician may have been well qualified in that role, you have outgrown that stage in your life. Time to move on. Likewise, if you have a toothache, you see a dentist, not a cardiologist. The same is true when it comes to investments. The counselor in whom you put your trust needs to be trained in the unique and individual challenges that present themselves once you advance toward the threshold of retirement, many of which have been presented for your consideration in this book.

True professionals will not mind your asking about certifications and qualifications, nor will they be insulted when you ask them about their compensation. To borrow a line from "The Godfather," it's business, not personal. When you see letters after the name on a business card, ask what they mean. They may look like alphabet soup to you, but they usually identify the bearer's training and specialization.

Don't be afraid to trust your impressions. You are a pretty good judge of character, aren't you? You would run the other way immediately if your doctor prescribed medication for you without asking a single question, wouldn't you? The same goes for your interview with a financial professional. The first time you meet, you should do most of the talking and the financial adviser should do most of the listening. The financial adviser who doesn't ask a lot of questions to get to know you and your unique financial situation is probably either incompetent or insensitive, neither of which bodes well for you in your search for the right financial adviser for you.

Education and certification are usually a good barometer of competence and trustworthiness, but not always. Consider the experience and the recommendations of others in that equation as well. Good communication between you and your adviser is essential. If you are dealing with a large firm with several employees, who will be your contact person? In our offices, it has become a ritual for our clients to become personally acquainted with the members of their financial advisory team and know what each one's responsibility is toward each client. Personal rapport means you are not likely to be treated as a number on a page of numbers, but as an individual. You want your adviser to connect your name immediately to your financial and retirement goals, wishes, dreams and desires.

Selecting the right adviser for you may require some legwork on your part, but the importance of the decision grows exponentially as the size of your holdings increases. Think of it as taking an expedition through unfamiliar territory, fraught with danger and adventure. You want someone who knows the land and can guide your steps expertly and safely, especially if you are retiring and are in the "red zone" of the financial playing field.

The Peak and Beyond

When we think of retirement as a journey up a slope characterized by challenging and unfamiliar footing, it's obvious that it's best to have a guide who has traveled that ground many times before and knows every little nuance of the trail. At the beginning of this book, we told you about Camelback Mountain, a Phoenix landmark that has become a perennial favorite of hikers in the area where we work and live. The mountain is tame at the start. Stair steps have been cut into the rock, and you think, "This is going to be easy." But the hard part comes when the terrain gets steeper, and you begin to notice your level of exertion increasing.

Some who come from cooler climates to Phoenix in the spring and summer discover what real heat is, too. Every year we hear about or read about someone who had to be rescued or airlifted down from Camelback because they underestimated the climb and got into some kind of trouble. It is dangerous in some places to leave the trail. One young hiker tumbled 40 feet to his death when he attempted to "free climb" the south side of the mountain.

Those steep sections going up can be even more treacherous coming back down. When you climb the Retirement Mountain, you will be immensely better off the more knowledge you gain of what lies ahead for you. A guide who knows the way is a good idea, too. And on a clear day, when the clouds are cotton balls against an aqua blue sky, and you can, or at least if feels like you can, see forever, you know what the fuss is all about and what awaits you was worth the climb.

The serious part of what we do is getting the numbers to go in the right direction for our clients. That's important, we realize. But that's not the fun part. The fun part is seeing our clients live the kind of life they had always dreamed of having in retirement, but weren't sure they could have. That's the part that makes it all worthwhile.

About the Authors

CALVIN GOETZ

Calvin Goetz is partner and co-founder of Strategy Financial Group, an Arizona financial advisory firm with offices in Phoenix and Tucson, a position to which he brings more than a decade of experience in wealth management and retirement income planning. His professional credentials include a Series 65 securities license, which enables him to offer investment advice and manage portfolios. He is also an Investment Adviser Representative of Strategy Financial Services, a Registered Investment Adviser firm.

An Arizona native originally from Tucson, Calvin is a proud graduate of Northern Arizona University. He now lives in the Arcadia neighborhood of Phoenix. A member of the board of directors for one-n-ten, Calvin is passionate about helping at-risk youth in Arizona. His dedication to serving the community also extends to his ongoing support of St. Mary's Food Bank and Ballet Arizona. When Calvin isn't helping his clients or supporting his community, he enjoys hiking Camelback Mountain and Piestewa Peak near his home, as well as yoga, running and weight training.

Family Life

Calvin's entrepreneurial spirt was inspired by his mother, Lorraine Goetz, who started her own daycare business after working as a preschool teacher for a number of years.

"My mother built that class from eight children up to 112," recalls Calvin. "She was a skilled and impassionate teacher who had excellent organization skills."

That passion for helping children learn, especially the fundamental values of sharing, communicating, listening and caring had an enduring impact on Calvin, who now teaches his clients the values of preparation and planning for their retirement.

Hard work and discipline were the cornerstones of the Goetz household. Calvin was with his mother every weekday when she opened the daycare at 6 a.m. and closed at 6 p.m. His father, Gary Goetz, who worked in the construction industry, woke at 4:30 a.m. every day so he could ensure a living for his family – a practice that taught Calvin the importance of accountability. Gary started his own masonry contracting business, which he operated for a number of years, and on weekends Calvin joined his father on jobs – he was not only building patios but also a strong work ethic. Gary later became a contractor for one of the largest construction firms in southern Arizona.

"Dad built hospitals, schools and shopping centers all over the state," says Calvin.

Calvin is the youngest of six children. When he was 9 years old, the Goetz family moved from Tucson to a 5-acre farm in Catalina, Arizona, about 20 miles to the north. They wanted to have an open area where they could grow their own food and raise livestock.

"At one point, we had dogs, chickens, turkeys and a giant tortoise," Calvin says, "as well as over 20 fruit trees."

Their home was so remote that Calvin had to bike or jog to visit friends, so he started running – something he naturally excelled at. When Calvin was a freshman at Canyon Del Oro High School he qualified for the varsity cross-country, track and field team. He was awarded a scholarship and graduated from Northern Arizona University where he set a personal best 5-kilometer record of 15 minutes flat for 3.1 miles.

Calvin considers both his parents to be excellent role models who taught him the value of industry, honesty and thrift. Growing up, Calvin would never have guessed that his parents' work experiences as teacher and builder would have such a powerful influence on his professional path, which has led him to become an educator on how to build retirement income plans.

Professional Life

Calvin started working when he was in high school. He did not know it then, but this early work experience combined with the entrepreneurial spirit and values of hard work and discipline from his parents would eventually develop a passion for helping people, specifically with the careful planning for their retirement.

Shortly after graduating from Northern Arizona University, Calvin worked for an estate planning firm, where he found the work interesting and rewarding, leading him in the direction of a career in financial services. He enjoyed helping families design and create estate plans, including wills, trusts, powers of attorney and living wills. He found fulfillment in helping people make the financial decisions that were associated with their estate plans. He eventually became a licensed investment adviser, and in 2010, Calvin co-founded the independent planning firm, Strategy Financial Group, where he serves his clients in a fiduciary role, specializing in conservative money management and retirement income planning.

"My most important achievements have been starting my business and continuing to serve and grow relationships with clients and their children," says Calvin.

Strategy Financial Group works with over 1,000 families in almost all 50 states. As a conservative wealth manager, Calvin strives to provide low-risk, personalized investment management designed to help retirees and those approaching retirement continue growing their wealth while maintaining their current lifestyles. Another goal is to help them plan effectively for the distribution of that wealth according to an integrated estate plan.

In recent years, Calvin has specialized in the intricate planning required for employer plans and 401(k) rollovers, helping corporate retirees efficiently transition their accumulated savings without unnecessary taxes, penalties or fees. Additionally, he specializes in creating tax-efficient, comprehensive financial plans.

Calvin is a member of the National Association of Insurance and Financial Advisors (NAIFA), an organization dedicated to positive legislative and regulatory advocacy within his profession. He is also a member of the prestigious Ed Slott IRA Advisor Group[SM], which awards membership to only the top 1 percent of financial professionals nationwide.

You may contact Calvin at:
Strategy Financial Group
3200 E Camelback Road
Suite 285
Phoenix, AZ 85018
602.343.9301
Toll free: 866.777.9219
cgoetz@strategyfinancialgroup.com
www.strategyfinancialgroup.com

Andrew Rafal is an investment and retirement adviser and a founding partner of Bayntree Wealth Advisors, a registered financial advisory firm with offices in Scottsdale, Peoria and Tucson, Arizona.

Andrew specializes in defensive investment risk management strategies with emphasis on building customized retirement plans, providing asset protection from market volatility, minimizing tax liability and maximizing wealth transfer. He is well known for his holistic, comprehensive approach to financial planning and upholds a "gain and retain" philosophy when it comes to retirement income planning.

Originally from Beachwood, Ohio, a suburb of Cleveland, Andrew now lives in Scottsdale, Arizona, just a short drive from the Bayntree Wealth office, which rests in the shadows of Camelback Mountain.

Family Life

Andrew credits his father, Ron Rafal, as the source of his strong work ethic.

"My father was told that he would never make it in college or in the business world," said Andrew. "He went on to become a successful CFO of a major health insurance company."

According to Andrew, his father didn't nag or brag; he just left good tracks to follow.

"He was all about being honest and true to your own ideals, concepts which he felt were the cornerstone of business success," Andrew said. "I try to follow that example in my professional life."

Andrew's mother, Debbie Malkin, left a different, although equally important imprint on his life – a love of reading and a creative/artsy side. As both of his parents would re-marry, Andrew notes that he benefitted from "two wonderful step-parents," Nancy Rafal and Alan Malkin, and a full house of siblings (one sister, three stepsisters and one stepbrother). Andrew calls his extended family his "support system," noting how much he relied on a strong network of family during his years growing up and remembers the entire clan getting together for unforgettable Thanksgivings over the years.

Andrew met his wife, Jules, on a night like any other in beautiful downtown Scottsdale.

"It was like the universe brought us together", he reminisced.

Andrew credits good communication and a true sense of partnership as the driving force behind their marriage, adding that their daughter, Winter, who is 10 years old at the time of this writing, is "Jules reincarnated."

Professional Life

Sports had a big influence on Andrew growing up.

"During my youth, I always enjoyed being competitive, and always strived to be on top," he says. "In sports, it's teamwork and common effort that make for a winning spirit. I have always enjoyed working as a team in business, also."

Andrew's first job was working at a grocery store owned by a family friend. Always the entrepreneur, when Andrew was in high school, he started his own window washing business, "with a little Toyota pickup truck and some gumption." Andrew and a couple of high school friends then started a photo-sharing business, which remained quite successful until he went off to college.

In his early 20s, Andrew began working with an independent insurance firm. During his five years there, he helped grow the company from five employees to more than 60. It was there that he began cultivating the relationships with clients that would be the foundation for his future with Bayntree Wealth Advisors.

When asked about his most important achievements in business, Andrew unhesitatingly points to the 250 families around the country who he has helped achieve their financial goals.

"I appreciate the trust they place in me," said Andrew. "They have hired me as their personal 'chief financial officer' and it is a responsibility I take very seriously."

He and his staff at Bayntree Wealth Advisors have seen their firm grow into a well-recognized brand that focuses on every aspect of retirement planning. Andrew enjoys his guest spots on "Good Morning Arizona" and "The Morning Scramble," where he provides financial and retirement tips.

Andrew is also a nationally recognized retirement planning contributor who has been featured in publications such as the Wall Street Journal, U.S. News and World Report, Forbes, USA Today and the Arizona Republic. He also provides financial education through speaking engagements at public events and at local colleges and universities.

Andrew is a member of National Association of Insurance and Financial Advisors (NAIFA) as well as Ed Slott's Elite IRA Advisor Group^{SM}, an organization of financial professionals dedicated to being leaders in the IRA industry. He graduated from the Richard T. Farmer School of Business at Miami University with a degree in finance.

Beyond the office, Andrew is a committed member of the community and is actively involved with EC70, a group dedicated to helping youth in Arizona overcome adversity. He enjoys traveling with Jules and Winter, as well as hiking and biking in the beautiful mountains of Arizona. An avid fan of the arts and theater, he and Winter have a standing date at the Nutcracker each December.

Andrew still roots for his hometown Cleveland teams and believes in his heart that one day he will see a championship brought to the shores of Lake Erie. Until then he will simply be just "waiting for next year."

You may contact Andrew at:
Bayntree Wealth Advisors
6720 N. Scottsdale Road
Suite 340
Scottsdale, AZ 85253
480.494.2750
arafal@bayntree.com
www.bayntree.com

49262849R00084

Made in the USA
Middletown, DE
21 June 2019